*Changes
From a
Sunset*

BY

Aileen Friedman

Editor
Franziska Annas
franziska.annas@gmail.com

Cartoon Illustration
Cara Friedman
ifriedaman@gmail.com

ISBN 13 – 978 0 620 52564 0

Author's Note

When I completed the first draft of this book in November
2010,
I could never have imagined how similar certain events in my
life would turn out similar to the way I wrote Chapter 22.
After discussing this turn of events with his family,
I do, with all sincerity & love, dedicate chapter 22 to:
Eugene Du Plessis
14.03.1984 – 06.09.2011
This world lost a beautiful soul
But Heaven has gained an angel.

With Love to:
My family,
I love you all so much, and I am so grateful
God has blessed me so immensely with a family
united in His Grace and Love.

To My mom Lucille
Alzheimer's may have taken your memory,
but it will never take my love for you

Special Thanks to:
Avril Hattingh & Hayley Janse Van Rensburg
& so many other friends
who have constantly encouraged me.

Contents

If we know the path our life is going to take, will we change it? Will we allow the hurt and pain to follow us on our journey through life? I doubt it. We will take only the happiness – consume it, multiply it, engulf it, relish it. But will we grow in such a perfect world? No, I believe we will become stagnant, immature, and unchallenged creatures, unworthy of the Lord and unable to be His servants.

Throughout our lives, filled with love, happiness, and tragedy, we all have a story to tell. But what will the ending bring? Will we hear the words, 'Welcome home, good and faithful servant,' or will we hang our heads in shame and regret not having used our fleeting lives to strengthen our faith in God? Whether we are happy and in love or faced with uncertainty and death, who do we rely on for strength, guidance, and comfort? With whom do we surround ourselves, and with whom do we spend our time? When our journey concludes, will it have the ending we desire?

There is no map to guide us on how to react to obstacles interrupting our desired peaceful existence. No matter how many times we imagine how we will deal with tragedy when the occasion arises, there are no rules. Our emotions run riot, taking control of our senses, and we cannot but submit to them – whether they compel us to panic, be calm, be hysterical, or be silent.

How do we move forward from deepest despair? Do we try to overcome it on our own, or do we wallow in self-pity, hindering any chance we might have of finding happiness again? Or do we immerse ourselves in the love of our family, friends, and God?

The choice is yours!

My life was perfect, happy, and simple. I was content and felt that nothing could go wrong in my world. Well, it did. My life got torn apart, and I stumbled into a conundrum of turmoil –

uncontrollably spiraling downwards and completely unable to keep everything from falling apart.

Now, what choice do I make?

<u>CHAPTER ONE</u>

Every Thursday evening, Cole, my partner of three years, my brother Eric, and I have dinner with my parents, Leon and Rose. They live just around the corner from my home in Gordons Bay, and on top of our regular family dinners, we see one another almost every day. Thursdays, however, are family night, and we are all expected to attend.

Eric is twenty-four and an utter nerd, permanently glued to his computer and understandably single. I have often tried to set him up with a friend, but he always finds an excuse to avoid the date, and I've subsequently given up. Like me, he is average height and dark hair, but unlike me, he dresses more sloppily than anyone else alive! My poor mother moaned at him throughout our childhood, but to no avail.

Cole is striking next to Eric – with his blonde hair, cheerful brown eyes, and a big smile. As an avid surfer, he is brown as a berry all year round. Since he is an accepted member of the family, he attends dinner on Thursdays without fail.

As always, I am greeted by the Jack Russell, aptly named Jack, when I walk into the house. My mother is busy in the kitchen, and my father is watching the news in the lounge.

'Hi Mum,' I say as I hug her and plant a kiss on her forehead.

'Hello, love! Eric isn't coming tonight. He phoned and gave some ridiculous excuse about working. He knows it's Thursday! Can't he just tell those people he works for that he has to have dinner with us?'

I hear the disappointment in her voice. She has never understood that people work longer than from nine to five these days.

'Is Cole coming? Don't tell me he's also working? What is this world coming to that no one appreciates family dinners anymore?'

'He'll be here, Mum,' I assure her before she feels the need to pop a pill or two.

I walk with her into the lounge, and she sits down across from my dad. I stand in the doorway and look at him, admiring what a genuine gentleman he is. Leon brims with kindness and love for Christ. He is very involved in the church, always visiting members, conducting Bible studies, and assisting various charity groups. On top of this, he still manages to run his own business. GB Tours is a tour company that takes tourists on daily and national tours, often doing business with the company I work for, Rio Adventures.

While I completed my degree, I worked part-time for my dad. Once I graduated as an accountant, he asked Mr. De Luca at Rio Adventures if a position came up, whether he would consider me. As it happened, a position was immediately available, and hence I started my career at Rio Adventures. I suppose I could have worked for my dad, but I wanted to see what else the world had to offer. Not much so far, but I'm happy. Besides, had my dad employed me, he would have had to get rid of someone else, and he'd never have been able to do that. He would rather starve than let an employee go, and in turn, his employees are equally loyal to him.

'Hi Dad, how was your day?'

'Busy as usual, but someone has to pay the bills, and fortunately, I have God on my side.' His usual reply.

I smile and cross the room to give him a hug, a kiss, and sit down next to him. We stare at the TV but don't pay much attention to the news. He puts his arm around me, and I snuggle into his chest. *I can never get too old for this.* If there is ever a place I feel safe and secure, it is here, in his arms. I don't even feel this safe with Cole. He kisses me tenderly on my head and asks how my day was.

'Okay,' I sigh.

Their home does not have an entrance hall; it is open plan, and you walk straight into the lounge from the front door. You'll see only the basics; no fancy furniture or ornaments.

'Material things don't get you into Heaven,' my dad always says.

It's still very cozy and homey, though, with family photos all over the place, and I love coming here.

A tap on the door, someone opens it, and walks in. Jack is the first to greet Cole.

'Hey, Jack, come here, boy,' he laughs, while he picks Jack up and lets him lick his face.

'Argh, no man! Cole! That's so disgusting!' I groan as I get up to greet him.

'Why? He's just saying hello.' He always lets Jack do this.

'Go and wash your face and hands,' I scold him like a school teacher.

He ignores me and greets my parents.

'Hi Rose, how are you today?' he asks, hugging her.

'Hello Cole, Eric isn't coming tonight! He has to work! Isn't dinner more important than work?' She looks at Cole reproachfully.

'I'm sure he would rather be here,' Cole replies politely.

He puts the jacket I asked him to bring for me over an armchair and moves in front of my dad to shake his hand.

'Hello Leon, how are you doing? Anything good happening in the world today?'

'Hello Cole, just negative news. Why they can't concentrate on the positive in the world is beyond me.'

Cole sits down in the armchair. My mum has made her way back to the kitchen and yells at me.

'Talia-May, get Cole and your father something to drink!'

My parents are the only ones who don't call me Tali. I wish they would; I've never liked my name.

'What do you want to drink, Dad, Cole?' I keep an eye on the TV.

They both ask for orange juice, and I force myself away from my dad's arm to fetch their drinks.

As I walk into the kitchen, my mother continues to complain about Eric's lack of commitment to the family. It is at times like this that I want to shake her and scream, 'So freaking what if he cannot make it! It's not the end of the world!'

I know I could never do that; she will dissolve into hysterics. She's been enjoying theatrics lately, and I've convinced myself it's because Eric and I aren't at home anymore, and she needs the attention.

I give my dad and Cole their orange juice when my mum announces that the food is ready. As always, there is food for a nation. Honestly, I think she cooks the entire week for this one evening – there's a leg of lamb, roast potatoes, mixed vegetables, and rice – all cooked the real old-fashioned way and served with thick gravy and a side salad. Then, after you can't eat another thing, out comes the dessert – ice cream and chocolate sauce today. She cooks like this regardless of the season.

'You've got to eat in the summer and the winter,' she will argue when we try to explain to her that it is just too hot for her food in summer.

'Looks good, Rose. I'm starving, so don't expect any leftovers. I never get food like this when I visit Tali,' Cole grins at me, and my mum beams.

'I taught her how to make food; she had to help make dinner every night as well as when we had guests. Don't let her tell you she can't cook!'

'I can cook,' I interrupt, 'I just choose not to!'

My mother gasps. 'Talia-May, how could you? I didn't raise you to neglect your duties. A woman's duty is to cook food for her man; what will Cole's parents think of you?'

Cole looks at me with a smirk, and I know he is going to use this as ammunition later on.

My dad looks at my mum, 'Let's eat and discuss Talia-May's cooking skills later, shall we?'

We sit down and hold hands as my father says grace. Dinner at home is always pleasant. We chat about our respective jobs, my mum continues complaining about Eric's absence, and finally, when all of us have eaten far too much, I muster up the energy to clear the table. Finally, we relax in the lounge, and once more, I snuggle into my dad's arms while Cole and my mum settle into the armchairs across from us.

We chat a little longer, and when my mum starts dozing in her chair, Cole and I head home. We say our goodbyes and walk to our respective cars; mine is a light-blue Ford Fiesta, and Cole's is a white 4x4.

'Think I must go straight home; got to get up at three to get to Mossel Bay,' Cole grumbles.

'Oh yes, I forgot you have to see your clients there this week.'

He puts his arms around me and holds me as if he will never let me go; then he kisses me gently. We know my parents are watching.

'I'll drive behind you; phone you when I get home.'

He kisses me again, then slowly lets me go and opens the car door for me.

Once I have my seatbelt on and the car started, he gets into his 4x4 and follows me home. On the way home, I cannot help but think what a good guy he is. There are not many men who will wait to move in together until marriage. We spend most nights together, but he knows what I want and never pushes the issue of moving in. I don't think I could be happier with anyone else. There weren't any sparks or fireworks, as some would insist upon when we met on the beach at a New Year's party. We discovered we could talk easily and have been together since. My dad always told me that God will find your soulmate, and you just have to trust in Him.

I pull into my driveway, get out of my car, and walk over to Cole. With his head out of the car window, his floppy blonde hair framing his face, he smiles.

'When I get back, we need to talk about your cooking duties, Tali,' and he bursts out laughing.

'I knew it,' I say, laughing too, 'you've probably been thinking about this all the way home.'

I lean into the window and kiss him goodnight.

'I love you,' he says.

'Love you too, please drive safely tomorrow.'

I park my car in the garage, let the automatic door close behind me, and go inside my homely rented cottage through the garage.

It can't be more than ten minutes before my phone rings.

'Just checking you're okay. Sleep tight, my love; I love you.'

'You sleep well too; I love you too.'

I can't help smiling. Trust my mother to give him some ammunition to get me to make food for him. He is always hungry.

CHAPTER TWO

It is three in the morning, and my phone blares out a song. I have a message. Reaching to find it, I grab the alarm clock, then my cup, and eventually something that feels like my phone. The message is from Cole, saying he is leaving. He will see me tomorrow; he hopes I have a good day and that he loves me.

Now it's the alarm clock that is blaring.

'Huh? No way! It can't be six thirty already?' I mumble to myself, 'No, not yet, how did it get to now so quickly? I still want to sleep, not fair…'

I groan, trying to find a reason not to get out of bed. I love my sleep and am most definitely not a morning person. I had fallen asleep with my phone in my hand, and the message from Cole was still open. Rereading it, I manage a smile and hit reply:

Drive safe, luv you so much, have a great day.

I suppose I had better get up, as I realize it's Friday, and immediately I feel better – nothing much ever happens at the office on a Friday. All the tour guides and sales staff are usually out on weekend camps and trips, and the office is peaceful.

I shuffle into the kitchen, put the kettle on for coffee, and then go to the bathroom. What to wear is occupying my half-awake brain, as is the case most mornings. Luckily for me, as long as we dress neatly, the De Lucases aren't fussy. While I wait for the water in the kettle to boil, I look in the mirror. I am of average height; my best feature is my long brunette hair, complemented by my green eyes. My mind wanders to the weather – it's going to be a fine twenty-eight degrees, with a slight breeze. I'm in an office all day, so I won't feel the heat. My pair of three-quarter black pants, an embroidered green sleeveless T-shirt, and black sandals should be perfect. Feeling comfortable after I've dressed, I have my coffee and leave for work. Just as I'm driving out of the driveway, I realize I've left my phone behind.

'You can be so stupid!' I reprimand myself.

It is almost seven o'clock, and if I waste any more time, I will be late for work.

Oh, please let there be no traffic today, I say a silent prayer.

Eventually, I am on my way to work, and fortunately, the traffic is okay. I allow myself to daydream a little. I wonder what I'll do tonight without Cole. My parents have church commitments; Sondra has her wedding to plan, and Cheri's husband Tian is home for a change.

Where does this leave me?

'Mm, maybe a movie and popcorn night all by myself,' I say aloud.

I'm sure I could call Garth and Merle and spend some time with them, but the idea of an 'alone night' sounds too good to miss. On my way home, I will stop off by the DVD store and rent a load of movies. Yes, this sounds like a great plan. Cole and I love watching movies, mostly comedies. As I completely avoid films with swearing, it is rather difficult for me to watch most movies.

Cole always says, 'That's the way it is today,' and I guess it is, but it still annoys me. Maybe an old classic is in order, something like *An Affair to Remember*. That sounds like a good one to watch on my own.

I am still listing movie options to myself when I reach the office, surrounded by high walls and a massive gate. The entrance has to be big to let the huge adventure Overlander trucks in and out. On days like today, there are three in the big cemented parking area, as well as two Jeeps. We all park our cars to the right of the building, under a shaded cover. I have to wait while one of the trucks reverses to load food, bedding, and equipment. I giggle and blow my hooter, not once, but three times. Some people jump in fright, while others yell at me, and I laugh harder. Then I see Josh De Luca, the owner, and my good humor vanishes instantly.

What will he think of my childish behavior?

As soon as the Overlander gets into position, I park my car and tell myself that that was not a very clever thing to do. I reach over to the passenger side, grab my laptop and bag, and get out slowly, hoping Josh will have left by the time I have to walk past everyone. It's not my lucky day. He is standing next to the truck, watching it being loaded and instructing the tour guides and Brett from marketing. I can never decide who is better-looking, Josh or Brett. Josh is dark with brown eyes and a lopsided yet lovely smile. About the same height as Brett, he is very well-built, but not so that you would notice immediately. He is exceptionally neat, very well-mannered, and has a quiet and kind air about him. Brett has similar features, but he's a real ladies' man. He cannot understand why the women at work are not interested in him, whereas out there in the world, he claims they fall at his feet.

My cheeks redden as I scurry to the entrance.

I mumble, 'Hi,' as I pass the truck.

'Hey, Tali!' They all laugh at my embarrassment.

I don't look up and head straight for the door, trying desperately to contain my laughter.

'Thanks, Tali, you certainly woke everyone up!'

I look up, shocked, realizing it is Josh who has spoken. He never joins in with any staff silliness, and I'd always thought he was far too aloof.

'You're welcome,' the words are out of my mouth before I know it.

What is wrong with me? I think, and cannot help but laugh out loud. I put my head down and push open the door.

Stupid, stupid woman, I think to myself.

Trust me to make Josh sociable.

'Morning, Miss Medeck,' says Booker as I whizz past him. His smile is also bigger than usual.

'Morning, Booker,' I mutter, hurrying on.

Mr. Booker, fondly known as Booker, is our security officer. I cannot think of a day when Booker isn't smiling. I asked him one day what his secret was, and he just smiled and said there was no point in complaining.

'If the first person you greeted was miserable in the workplace, then how are you supposed to have a good day, Miss Medeck?'

He is small for a security officer, but can run like the wind, even at fifty-nine years old. I once saw him run in a race against the rest of the male staff at a team-building event, and he beat them hands down.

I wait for the elevator in the foyer of Rio Adventures. It's a spacious room, airy and light, and filled with healthy-looking tropical plants. The building consists of four floors, and I'm on the third. The first three floors are all open-plan offices, except for the fourth – the De Lucas' offices – Mr. Gavino De Luca and his son Giosia, whom everyone calls Josh, are on the top floor.

While I wait, I play my usual guessing game – which of the two elevators will win the lucky prize and take me to my floor? To further amuse myself, I add a different accent to my thoughts each time. The Italian accent I attempt does not go down well, but at least I can laugh at myself. I don't dare look around, and at the same time, I battle not to laugh. Elevator Number One arrives.

'Too bad, Number Two,' I say, and step in, hoping no one will join me.

My luck is just not in today. Shelly, one of the tour guides, comes running to catch it.

I'm just grateful it's not Josh. Shelly is so tiny that it's hard to believe she could guide anyone anywhere, but she has a surprising amount of strength and stamina.

'Oh Tali, that was so fantastic!' She laughs.

'Glad I can amuse you,' I say, half sarcastically.

'We all got such a fright, but to top it all, Josh joined in! Bet you didn't see that one coming?'

She's so bubbly it's hard not to laugh.

'I was there, remember? If only I had seen him. Oh my word, what a start to the day. Suppose I will get a memo from the De Lucas, "NO HOOTING," it'll say.'

Shelly bursts out laughing again, and as the doors are about to shut, Greg glides into the elevator. He is well over six feet tall, with prematurely grey hair, and always wears jeans, a golf shirt, and sneakers, regardless of the weather. You never notice him until he is right next to you – he never seems to walk; he glides, and so softly too. Shelly gets out on the first floor, where all the tour guides and sales staff work, and Greg on the second, in the marketing department.

Sondra and Cheri are at the coffee machine already, and I throw my laptop and bag on my desk and make a beeline to join them. They both look at me with surprise written on their faces. Sondra is our receptionist and Cheri's assistant – she is twenty-five years old and will be getting married in a few months. Her wispy blonde hair and freckled face, matched with grey eyes and her average height and build, make her far from perfect – but to her fiancé, Neville, and me, she is. Cheri, our payroll manageress, is thirty-two years old, married, and has a five-year-old son. Her husband Tian is always away on business, so Cheri and little Tian are usually alone. She is stunning – a brunette with dark eyes and the longest lashes I've ever seen. In her younger days, she must have had men lining up to be with her.

'What on earth's wrong with you, what happened?' Cheri asks, full of concern.

'Cole proposed?' Sondra is always ready to pop the champagne.

'Oh, I wish,' I grin and tell them what happened.

'Oh, my word, and Josh made fun of you and joined in with everyone's laughter? That has got to be a first!'

'Thanks for reminding me I've corrupted the boss.'

Back at my desk, I realize it's not such a big issue, but because Josh hardly speaks to anyone about anything other than business, it's a surprise. I jump with fright when the phone rings, and my heart starts racing as I immediately think it might be De Luca ready to scold me. Sondra and Cheri have shared my thoughts and freeze as I lift the receiver.

'Tali speaking,' I say as calmly as I can.

'Hello, sunshine!' Cole! My heart skips a dozen beats just at the sound of his voice, but at this point, it might just be from relief.

'Oh, I'm so glad it's you,' and I tell him about my eventful morning.

Sondra and Cheri look puzzled until I point at the phone and mouth, 'Cole.'

'Oh my goodness, love, I wish I'd seen that. I can just imagine the shade of red your face was - a good way to start your day! And here I was thinking you weren't going to have any fun without me.'

'So, how's your day going?' I change the subject.

'Well, clearly not as good as yours, but I've got to see old Frederick in about fifteen minutes. He is the first on the list for the day – best to get the worst over and done with.'

Cole is a freelance sports writer, which means that he is often away for interviews. Not surprisingly, he focuses mostly on surfers.

'How come you didn't phone me on my cell phone?'

It has dawned on me that he is calling my landline, which is unusual.

'Take a look, and you'll probably find it's flat; I've left you a few nice messages,' he teases.

I take my phone out of its cover and sigh.

'Oh no, I'm such an idiot, this is so typical of me.'

'What've you got planned for tonight? Big girls' night out while the cat's away, hmmm?'

'No, it's a one-girl-night tonight. I'm going to get some real old classic chick flicks, a huge bowl of popcorn, and spend quality time with my couch. I'm going to have some real alone time.'

'Can't I crash your party?' He laughs, says he has to go, and promises to leave some more sweet messages on my phone.

'You know he is the nicest guy in the world,' I coo to Sondra and Cheri.

'So, when are you going to tie the knot?' asks Cheri, 'It's about time!'

'Oh, I don't know. It's good the way it is, why mess with it?'

I know this is not exactly true. Deep down, I want the whole wedding day thing, but I'm comfortable with the way things are, and I would rather have Cole this way than not at all.

'Ooh, talking about weddings…' Sondra's eyes light up as they always do when she's going to talk about hers. 'The bridesmaid and flower girl dresses are so gorgeous, and just about everyone we invited is going to be there, so we're looking at about seventy guests – which is what we budgeted for!'

'Have the De Lucases replied?' Cheri asks.

We were surprised when Sondra said she'd invited them, because, like the rest of us, she has no interest in them outside of business.

'No, they still haven't. But we know they won't come, so we haven't even added them to the guest list.'

'It still confounds me as to why you invited them in the first place, Sondra,' Cheri raises her neatly shaped eyebrows.

'Well, if they did come, I would get one very expensive present!' Sondra grins.

'You're evil,' I laugh.

'Hey, do you know if the fax from Select Foods has come through yet?' I turn to Sondra, suddenly realizing I have something called work to do.

CHAPTER THREE

On the way home, I stop at Just DVDs and take out *An Affair to Remember*, *Hope Floats*, *The Lake House*, and *Chocolat*. An alone night, I smile to myself.

One of the reasons I rent my cottage is that it provides good security. A wooden fence surrounds it, with an intercom for visitors, and the door from the garage leads directly into the open-plan lounge, kitchen, and dining room. I put my bag, laptop, and keys down on the table by the door and head for the kitchen. It is a one-bedroom house, so there is a very narrow, short passage leading to the bedroom on the left and to the bathroom through a door on the right. A quaint garden borders the house in which I spend lots of my time tending to the flowers. I've tried growing vegetables, but can't seem to get the hang of it. The house is small but cozy, and like my parents, I have photos gracing almost every wall.

While the popcorn pops, I make my way to the couch, a huge sofa bed decorated with comfy cushions. There's no space for other chairs, and just about enough room for a coffee table and a TV on a stand in front of the wall. The big sliding doors on either side of the room mean it's well-lit, and it's probably my favorite spot in the house. Just as I'm getting comfortable, I realize my phone is flat and still in my bag. I get up again, put the phone on charge in my room, grab the popcorn off the stove, put it into a bowl, and finally snuggle up on the couch to watch *Chocolat*.

Ah, bliss, I think to myself.

In the early hours of the morning, I finish watching the last of the DVDs. I am not very tired, but I know that if I don't go to sleep now, I never will.

At nine o'clock, I jump in fright when I hear the front door open. Groggy and half asleep, I am suddenly being held. Cole is home.

'Mm, this is the best way to wake up,' I murmur, 'why didn't you call to say what time you were getting here?'

'Put your phone on and check how many messages you have, my dear.'
'Oh goodness, I forgot about it, oh I'm so sorry.'
I quickly run to my room, take my phone off the charger, and switch it on. There are sixteen messages from Cole and three from my mother.
'I'm so sorry I forgot to put it on! Thank goodness you're not a possessive boyfriend – this probably would have pushed you over the edge!' I laugh.
We snuggle up on the couch; I can tell the traveling has tired him out, and before long, we are both asleep.
It is evening when we wake up; I cannot believe we've slept away an entire day, and Cole is even more horrified than I am.
'The surf was supposed to be great today,' is all he can say.
'What are we going to do for dinner? And don't even think about me cooking up a storm!' I say before he can remind me of my mother's famous words.
'Why don't we go to Rumps?'
I eagerly agree, as Rumps is our favorite restaurant in the Strand, and we eat there at least twice a week. We shower hurriedly, change, and head out for dinner.
As always, we have a great time at Rumps. We almost always have the He-Man steak, which comes with either mushroom or pepper sauce, a baked potato with sour cream, a side salad, and vegetables. The steaks are enormous, which means I never finish mine. Cole, of course, takes great pleasure in finishing it for me. After we've eaten, we usually sit in the lounge area and relax, chatting with other guests or the young American couple who own the place. The restaurant has a great vibe and is very family-oriented, relaxing, and extremely popular. So much so that we sometimes have to wait up to an hour for a table, but it's always worth it.
As usual, we are the last people to leave.
While we slowly walk to the car, Cole blurts out, 'We should get married here when we eventually do.'
My jaw drops, and I stop in my tracks and stare at him.
'Um, that is out of the blue!' I can't gulp back my words and mutter, 'Stupid!'

'Yeah, I know,' he laughs, and I think he's just as surprised at what he said as I am.

'But it would be perfect, don't you think?' He blushes, 'I mean, we love the place, and we've always said we don't want lots of people at our wedding.'

'Venue, check,' I make a ticking motion with my left hand and put my other arm around him. He holds me tightly. Can't say I minded one bit.

We get into his car with smiles on our faces, and I wonder if every time we come here from now on, we will discuss wedding plans. It's a quiet drive home; both of us are occupied with our thoughts. I would take a wager that both our thoughts are on the same thing – a wedding! It made me feel a little nervous as it suddenly dawns on me that Cole might propose sometime soon.

How will he do it? I wonder. *Will he get down on one knee and give me the big speech? Probably not; that's so unlike him. No, he'll probably ask me while we're lying in bed, and he will have hidden the ring under the pillow. Or maybe while we're walking on the beach on a hot summer's evening.*

My mind plays out one scenario after another, and as I decide which way I prefer, I'm brought back to reality when we arrive at my house.

Once inside, I put the water on to boil. Cole comes up behind me, puts his arms around me, and starts kissing my neck.

Oh no, not in the kitchen! He's going to propose in the kitchen! That's just so unromantic!

'I'm sorry,' he says softly in my ear.

'For what?' I'm a little confused, and turn around to look him in the eyes; I'm not expecting an apology.

'I shouldn't have said anything about a wedding. Silly of me to blurt out something like that; I can see it's made you a little nervous.'

How perceptive is he?

'Don't be sorry. Don't ever be sorry about something like that. I'm glad you said it. At least, I know you don't plan on leaving me, and, you know, I quite like the idea. I think it will be perfect too.'

'Where would I go, love? You know the rest of my life is with you. I love you like crazy.'
He holds my face in his hands and kisses my forehead softly, then moves on to my nose and my lips.
Then he pulls me closer and whispers, 'Forget the Horlicks…'

CHAPTER FOUR

The next few weeks fly by; I go to work, have dinner with my parents, and on weekends, I spend time with Cole. I'm pleased with the peaceful and uneventful track my life is on. Of course, at work, nothing is peaceful for long, and there is always someone who seems to need my attention.

It is now two weeks before Sondra's wedding, and this consumes our conversations at the office. Today is no different. At lunch, we roll our chairs over to the coffee machine, and in between sips of coffee and bites of cheese croissants, we chat nonstop. Sondra can't stop talking about the flowers that are suddenly out of season; it's a wonder she eats any food, she rants so much! Suddenly, her phone rings.

She puts her coffee and croissant down, wipes her hands on her serviette, and rolls her chair to her desk.

'Admin, Sondra speaking,' she says, annoyed.

We dislike it when our lunch is interrupted. Her face reddens, and she scowls at us. Cheri and I stop chattering and watch her, trying to gauge who she is speaking to.

'Oh, um, no, that's not a problem.'

Cheri and I snicker at her obvious discomfort.

'Oh, you would? Oh, no, that won't be any problem at all. I feel honored that you want to be there. Thank you very much,' her voice rises a notch, and she rolls her eyes at us.

Cheri and I pretend to look shocked and start giggling like schoolgirls. We wait for her to put the phone down before asking questions impatiently. Sondra is clearly agitated.

'So? What was all that about? Come on, tell us, we're dying to know!' Cheri demands, but Sondra just stares at her desk for a few seconds.

Sondra looks up at us, bewildered, and replies slowly, 'Josh De Luca accepted my wedding invitation; he is coming to my wedding, and he apologizes for replying so late, but he would love to be there.'

'Oh my goodness!' Cheri and I chorus and burst out laughing.

'Is that all? You wanted to invite him, and now maybe you'll get that expensive present! After all, isn't that the only reason you invited him?'

Cheri and I continue laughing. It's just so funny to see Sondra's face. The De Lucases haven't attended any staff member's wedding before, and there have been at least three.

'So, where are you going to seat him? Oh, wait, is he bringing a date? I wonder who it will be.' I'm very curious. 'You'd better put him at the main table since he will be bringing such an expensive present.'

Cheri can't contain herself any longer, and tears stream down her face as she crumples into her chair from laughter.

Sondra glares at us, 'Go ahead and laugh, you two; this is the very last thing I expected! Oh goodness! Where do I seat him? Can you imagine him sitting anywhere near my Aunt Glenda? She will tell him every sordid detail of my life. Oh, why did I send out that invitation?'

Cheri and I both feel her anxiety, but that does not stop us from laughing. Much later, when we realize that our lunch has been almost two hours – thanks to Josh – we dutifully try to concentrate on our work. Sondra, however, spends the rest of the day with her guest list, working out the seating arrangements. There are certain family members she wants to keep apart from one another and, at the same time, separate from everyone else.

'Put them in the back,' I point to the guest list, 'or seat them with you.'

Cheri and I comment at every chance we get, but Sondra is not impressed with our lack of sympathy.

On my way home from work, I feel bad for laughing at Sondra, but it was just too funny to pass up! I also can't stop wondering why Josh even wants to be at the wedding. Why the change of heart? Sondra is nothing to him but a junior employee. Why, when he has never attended any of the other weddings, does he want to go to hers? Poor Sondra, however, stressed she was before today about getting married; she must be really worried now. She keeps reminding Cheri and me about how her family gets carried away at functions, and what will Josh think of her when she returns to work after the honeymoon? I told her all day there's no point in worrying about it – he has no right to judge her or her family, and if he wants to be there, then he had better accept her family.

Cole's apartment is a bachelor's apartment, one road up from Strand Beach. Furniture is sparse as it is not a priority for him. As long as he has a bed to sleep in and a couch to sit on, he is happy. I love his flat. It's so casual and relaxing; there's a couch, two beanbags, a TV on the coffee table, and his surfboards adorn all the walls. The enclosed balcony, which serves as his bedroom, gets extremely hot in the summer, as does the kitchenette. He has all the basics, and, unlike most bachelor's, keeps everything surprisingly neat. He is out surfing when I arrive, so I make myself comfortable on the couch in front of the TV and think about what we can make for dinner.
It is, at least, half an hour later when a wet Cole walks in at the door, smelling of salt and surf. I love the smell and rush over to greet him. He's not very happy because there were no waves, but after I mention my day, he's smiling again. While he showers, I chop some vegetables.
Cole can fry the steak after his shower; I think to myself, which he dutifully does once he's clean, fresh, and human-smelling again.
I recite Sondra's woes in more detail and giggle while I tell him how funny Cheri and I found everything. Somehow, most men don't seem to find the same things funny that women do, but he listens intently and laughs at all the right places.
'Shame, you women are cruel. So why do you think Josh is suddenly so interested in his staff?' he asks, flipping the steak over and smoking out the whole apartment.
'Open the windows and the door,' I say, and do it myself.
'I don't know; it's weird, we've seen and heard more of him in this last week than we have the entire year.'
'Maybe he's looking for friends,' Cole says jokingly.
'With their money, I doubt he needs to look for friends.' I know I shouldn't have said that.
'Don't be nasty,' Cole smacks me lightly on my bum.
We sit down on the couch and, as we eat, Cole tells me about an old sportswriter he interviewed with today. Nick Drummond

was once a renowned horse race commentator. I find it fascinating, and we chat about it at length, especially since Sport Today will publish it in their next issue.

'It's going to be a brilliant article; I know it!' I assure him.

'The most interesting part of his whole life story is how he committed his life to God and the work he has done since then,' Cole looks at me seriously.

'Really?' I cannot help the surprise in my voice.

'Yeah, you'd be surprised at the number of sports celebs that are Christians, and do fantastic work. We don't publish that, though, I mean, it's not what our readers are interested in, you know.'

'That's ridiculous!'

'No, really, the editors won't publish it. They claim that anything to do with Christianity belongs in a Christian magazine and not ours.'

'And the other Christian sports celebs, do you ever discuss Christianity with them, like besides Nick Drummond?'

'Oh sure, and it's all fascinating. I usually share both our backgrounds with them, and then they offer a lot of advice – always telling me to give God a chance and to hold on to you! That's when I tell them you're a dragon with missing teeth!'

He laughs, and I punch him lightly on the arm, telling him how horrible he is, but at the same time, I join in his laughter. I realize he is trying to make light of the conversation.

'What do you say to them when they tell you that?'

'Tell me what?'

'You know when they tell you to change your life.'

'Oh, well, I tell them I do think about it, and that I'm sure it will happen one day. And then they always say you never know when your time is up, and it might be too late.'

'So what do you think about that?' I am curious and eager to keep this conversation going.

'Well, I do think about it, and I know your church seems to have the right answers. I just think I should know a bit more before I make any commitment. I think one should take it very seriously. You know, it's not something you can just change your mind about when you feel like it at a later stage.'

I am hesitant to push this, but at the same time, I want to encourage his search.

'Well, if you want to find out more, I'll help you, okay, or I can ask someone else to study with you when you're ready, whatever you prefer. Just ask, okay?'

'Thanks, love, if anyone is going to study with me, it'll be you and your dad.'

We smile at each other, and I know to leave the subject there.

We take our dishes to the kitchen and clean up. Cole has meetings with editors, publishers, and other not-so-important people tomorrow and still has a lot of work to do, so I stay for another two hours and then head home. My thoughts are much occupied with our conversation. I'm happy Cole is, at least, thinking about his life. Maybe I will go back to church on Sunday. My parents will probably pass out from the shock.

CHAPTER FIVE

'Morning, Booker!' I exclaim as I walk into the office building. It's a bit chilly this morning, so I'm wearing blue jeans, a red long-sleeve top, a colorful scarf, and black pumps.

'Morning, Miss Medeck!' He returns my smile with an even bigger one.

I'm already at the elevators before he can even ask me how I am or start up a conversation. I'm still very preoccupied with last night's conversation and cannot understand why it is bothering me so much.

'Number Two today, come on Number Two,' I say to myself in a French accent.

'Good morning, Tali,' a soft voice says from behind me.

I nearly jump out of my skin and am about to scold Greg for creeping up on me again when I notice it's Josh.

Oh no, not again, why is he around so much lately? I think to myself, panicking for no apparent reason – except that he's my boss, and I'm silly, I guess.

'Um, good morning, Josh, how are you?'

Ah, well done, Number Two, I think, as we step into the elevator side by side.

Josh is dressed casually today in jeans and a light blue golf shirt – more casually than I think I've ever seen him.

'I'm so sorry for startling you like that. I'm fine, thank you, and you?' He looks at me apologetically.

'Well, thanks,' I don't know what else to say, so I press our respective floor buttons and stare at the elevator doors.

I must have a "Let's embarrass Tali" button in my brain that only switches on at the most inconvenient of times.

Before I can stop myself, I blurt out, 'They should put cartoons on the doors so you can amuse yourself while you're riding in the elevator!'

I feel my face flush, and a heat creeps from my neck into my cheeks.

What is wrong with me? What am I thinking? Why do I always blurt out such crazy things? Why does he always have to be around when I do?

He lets out a chuckle, 'You're right! I think I'll get Brett and Greg onto it right away.'

I do not dare look at him, 'I didn't mean that, uh, don't take me seriously!'

'But it's a good idea, don't you think?'

I'm out of the elevator before the doors are fully open, and relieved to be the first one in the office, dumping my bag on my desk, putting the coffee on, and staring out the window. Staring into nothingness always seems to calm me down.

The elevator doors open, and Sondra and Cheri come strolling into the office.

'Hi, ladies, coffee's almost ready,' I pipe up.

'Hey, Tali!' They reply in unison.

I tell them about my stupid comment in the elevator and, like Josh, they think it's a great idea.

'But it's so true, Tali! I never know where to look, especially if it's just one other person and me – it's always so uncomfortable!' Cheri sounds excited.

'Well, you're welcome to raise it at the next staff meeting as your idea,' I mutter grumpily.

'When I told Neville about the phone call, he couldn't believe Josh is coming to the wedding. He says if we don't get a lot of money, he's going to kick him out!' Sondra laughs as she mimics Neville's gruff voice. We all chuckle as we envisage Neville giving Josh the boot.

'Oh, by the way, we're seating him with you guys,' Sondra smirks.

'Oh no! No, no, no, you can't do that! What have we ever done to you?' I squeal, 'You can't be serious; you're joking, right?'

'Nope, sorry, it's the only table that has an extra seat. Oh, and guess what? He isn't bringing a date!' Sondra laughs at our astonishment, elated at her revenge for our being so unsympathetic the previous day.

'No ways! Josh is not bringing a date?' Cheri is as surprised as I am.

'He sent me an internal email and never gave an explanation.'

'Sondra, this is not funny at all! How are we supposed to entertain him for a whole day? If he, at least, had a date, he'd be occupied with her.' The thought of spending almost an entire day with my boss and such a strange guy at that mortifies me.

Sondra trots off to the ladies', and Cheri grabs the opportunity to ask me about the hen party.

'Did you get the email about Saturday night?'

'Yes, it's going to be crazy by the sounds of it. It seems her family knows how to party!' I roll my eyes.

'I know, and you and I will be a pair of wet blankets among them, that's for sure.'

I nod, 'At least, they don't know us, so we can just hang around in the background and watch them torture her. It'll be our revenge on her for making us sit with Josh!'

Cheri laughs and looks away as Sondra walks back into the office.

We get on with our work, and it turns out to be one of those frustrating days where nothing seems to go right. The phones ring nonstop, and Clyde, one of the tour guides, is an absolute pain. We rarely have much to do with the tour guides, as June usually handles them, but today Clyde is on a rampage. According to him, he isn't paid enough commission, and he spends most of the day arguing with us about it.

'What an ass,' Cheri, who hardly ever calls people names, is extremely annoyed.

'Wow, is that man rude!' Sondra adds.

We decide to go out for lunch to get out of the office for a while. Arriving at our usual coffee shop, Shapes, we order cappuccinos and salmon salads from a trainee waiter. He has to come back three times to confirm our orders, and then still gets mine wrong! I don't mind new waiters, but why today of all days? Eventually, after waiting for an hour, we are disappointed and irritated and ask for takeaways.

Back at the office, we've all received a memo for the next staff meeting, Tuesday next week at nine o'clock.

'Oh, good grief! What else? Next thing, De Luca himself will walk in and make our day complete!' I groan while I eat my salad at my desk.

'Be quiet! Please don't hex the day any more than it already has been,' Sondra says with her mouth full of food.

I open my inbox to check for emails and find one from Denise, Sondra's bridesmaid, who is organizing the hen party. She wants Cheri and me to create a diversion on Saturday to make sure Sondra is surprised. She suggests we tell Sondra we need a girls' night out, do something with her, and then arrive at Shelter, where they'll all be waiting. Shelter is a pleasant and respectable nightclub in Somerset West, and thankfully, they are very particular about who they allow in. The idea is to have a few drinks there, embarrass Sondra as much as possible, and then go to Denise's house for the rest of the evening. Cheri coughs, and I look up at her. By the look on her face, I can tell she has just read the same email.

Cheri sends me a Skype message:

We can make today an excuse for a girls' night out on Sat. I will go to the ladies room now and phone Neville to make sure he is on board with the plan.

I look up again and nod. Cheri leaves with her phone in her pocket, and after a few minutes returns and Skypes me again:

Denise already put him in the picture.

'Wow, I think that we need a good ladies' night out after today's chaos!'

'Oh, for sure! Today has been the absolute pits!' I reply with a straight face.

Sondra nods, 'Sounds great, let me just check with my hubby-to-be.'

Cheri picks up her phone, chats with Tian, and checks that he will be available to watch little Tian. She's already spoken to him in the ladies', so he's just playing along.

'Okay, that's me sorted for Saturday, so where should we go?'

Sondra is still on the phone with Neville, and he seems to be enjoying the little game. He tells Sondra that they already have a barbecue with his parents arranged, but he will see if he can cancel it. He waits about half an hour and then phones her back, confirming that he's managed to cancel, as long as they barbecue on Sunday. Neville is not interested in having a bachelor party, but all the men are getting together for a barbecue at his house on Saturday.

I ring Cole, and then we're all sorted.

'How about Shelter?' Sondra suggests, 'I love that place.'

Cheri Skype's me:

Do you think she knows??

I reply:

I don't think so! She loves the place, so it's no surprise she wants to go there!

I hear Cheri sigh:

Yeah, that's true, thank goodness we don't have to convince her to go somewhere else, and make it too obvious.

I look up at Cheri and grin.

'Okay, awesome Shelter it is then! Saturday, beware; these three ladies need some serious chilling time!' I exclaim while making cheering motions with my arms and acting super excited about the upcoming night out.

I am looking forward to the party, though, because if Sondra's family is as crazy as she makes them out to be, it's going to be one very entertaining night.

As I'm about to leave the office, my phone rings.

'Tali speaking, hello?'

'Guess what? Eric is bringing his girlfriend to meet us tonight. My Eric finally has a girlfriend, and I bet she's perfect for him!' My mum is so excited that she doesn't even say hello.

I can see my mother is already planning their wedding.

'You're joking? What did he do, get his laptop to walk?' I burst out laughing at my joke.

'Oh, that is not a nice thing to say, Talia-May. Now don't be late, we don't want to give her a bad impression of our family, okay?'

'Oh, Mother, please! She won't be royalty; she's probably a computer nerd just like he is.'

'See you just now,' she says and puts the phone down.

I rattle everything off to Sondra and Cheri, who at least appreciated my laptop joke, and as we walk to our cars, we all agree she's a computer nerd too.

When I arrive at my parents' house, I'm surprised to see Eric's car parked outside already. He never gets here before I do. I can hear my mum laughing as I approach the front door. As I reach the door, it opens for me, and my beaming mum, whose eyes are sparkling, welcomes me. She does not give me the chance to say hello, let alone a hug or a kiss.

'Eric is here,' she gushes, 'and he's brought his girlfriend for dinner to meet us.'

'Eric, you little sneak!' I call out to him as I brush past my mum.

I look at my brother and see a huge smile on his face and a twinkle in his eyes. He looks completely over the moon.

'So? When did all this happen? And why didn't you ever say anything to me?' I pat him teasingly on the shoulder and turn to the woman next to him.

'Hi there, I'm Tali,' I say as I put my arms out to hug her.

'Talia-May is her proper name,' my mother looks pointedly at me.

'Tali, this is Judith, Judith, this is my sister Tali – watch out for her, she bites!' He introduces us as Judith hugs me back.

'And when we ladies get together, we all become vampires!' Judith retaliates and grins at me.

She has a sweet voice and an almost angelic smile. She is beautiful, to say the least, with porcelain skin and long blonde hair. I cannot make out whether her eyes are blue or green.

'Oh no! One second with my sister and already she has corrupted you!' Eric laughs and then groans as I punch his arm.

'Talia-May! What will Judith think of us? We are not violent people!' My mum is so desperate to make a good impression.

Judith smiles, 'That's okay, Rose, my brother and I play-fight all the time, and he's older and much bigger than me, so I always lose!'

The front door bangs, and Cole saunters in. I've completely forgotten to tell him the good news, so the look on his face is incredulous.

'Now here is a perfect man, Judith, but hands off – he's mine forever!' I laugh as I take Cole by the hand.

'Cole, please meet Judith, Eric's girlfriend! Judith, this is Cole.'

'Eric, nice!' He pats Eric on the back and turns to Judith, 'Pleased to meet you, Judith. Good evening, Leon, you've got a full house tonight, I see.' Cole greets my dad with impeccable manners as always.

'Yes, and I hope we'll get to eat sometime soon. I'm starving.' My dad grins.

'Oh, shush, do you ever go hungry?' My mum jokingly retorts. I offer everyone some juice, and we all chat about our day. Most of the questions, however, are directed at Judith, as we're all dying to find out more about her. Eric is glowing. It's so cute to see my little brother so smitten. We find out that Judith is a dancer and teaches at a studio in Somerset West. She met Eric at a mutual friend's house two months ago. They became friends on Facebook, went on coffee dates that progressed into dinner dates, and their relationship developed from there. Trust Eric to keep this a secret from us for so long.

The evening goes smoothly, and by the time we leave, it is clear to everyone, even to the photos on the walls, that Eric and Judith are well-suited to each other. I am truly happy for him.

Cole is staying the night at my place, and while I make us both a cup of Horlicks, I tell him about our plans for Sondra's hen party.

'Cheri says we're going to be like a pair of wet blankets in comparison to all Sondra's crazy relations. You know she and I aren't the biggest party animals, so I hope they don't get all offended if we don't get drunk and out of control.'

'If they're like that, then they won't know the difference! Us men, we will behave as we always do,' is Cole's mocking reply.

'Isn't Judith lovely? I can't believe Eric kept her a secret for so long. My mother is so ecstatic that her little boy has finally got himself a girlfriend! Shame, it's so sweet to see her so happy for her children. I reckon she's planned his wedding already.'

Cole laughs 'I don't think I've ever seen your mum so excited; she was like a bubble about to burst. Eric is so in love, the poor guy.'

'Well, I think they're perfect for each other. I know it is too soon to say, but they look like they've been together forever. We must go out together sometime soon.'

'Oh, you're just nosey and want to find out all about her life history,' Cole teases.

'That's not true; you're nasty! I do want to get to know her, of course, I do, but not in that sense.' I pretend to look offended, though I know he's just joking.
I suppose he is right in a way; I am curious about her. After all, it is my little brother.

CHAPTER SIX

Saturday arrives on cue. I have to pick Cheri and Sondra up at six o'clock in the evening, and it's now only ten in the morning. Cole left early this morning to go surfing and will head to Neville's house later for the barbecue.

After I have had my hair done, I pop into the baby shop next door to the hairdresser and buy my friend Merle a gift for her baby. She is seven months pregnant, and I can't believe we still have two whole months to wait to meet the little guy.

Garth, Merle's husband, and Cole have been friends almost all their lives. They met at the age of seven when they lived next door to each other. They remained steadfast friends throughout school and afterward went abroad to Bali together in search of any remote beach with monstrous waves. Cole was Garth's best man when he and Merle got married last year after they'd been dating for four years. Garth is the same height and build as Cole, but has sharper features, brown eyes, and is bald – not because he is losing his hair, but because he prefers it that way. Merle, when she isn't pregnant, is slightly overweight, of my height, and has long, thick, black hair, hazel eyes, and a happy, round face.

We get along so well; it's as though all four of us grew up together. It was at their New Year's Eve beach party that Cole and I met – a fact they never let us forget! Almost every time we see them, Garth will tell us how eternally grateful we should be to them for making our union possible – and that we need to shower them with gifts to continually show our gratitude!

Garth and Merle greet me warmly when I arrive. Merle is thrilled with the pram set I bought, which, naturally, has Winnie the Pooh motifs all over it.

'Don't you ever buy anything without Pooh on it? I'd better warn Cole now that his child, whenever that happens, will be a Winnie the Pooh replica!' Garth always finds his comments very funny and proceeds to laugh alone at his joke.

'Oh, Garth, but it's all so cute! I would buy out the whole store if I could. I dread even to think what I'm going to be like when I have my child – whenever that happens.' I emphasize the "whenever that happens" as he did.

Over coffee, we chat about the hen party, but mostly about the baby's due date.
'Since we know it's a boy, Merle and I have decided to name him Cole.' Garth gets up from his seat for no apparent reason.
'Oh really? Oh, that's just so wonderful! Cole is going to be so touched. Have you told him yet?' I cannot help the lump in my throat and the tears that well up in my eyes.
'No, not yet, and don't you go and say anything until we do.' Garth sounds very firm.
'I won't, you know I wouldn't! Thanks, guys! That's so special. Little Cole Junior.'
I tenderly touch Merle's tummy, which is so huge that she's begun to waddle when she walks! I reach out to hug her and Cole Junior, and she pats my back, and then stands up and gives me a proper hug.
'So, why don't I get a hug? He's my child too, hey?' Garth pretends to look upset.
'Oh, come here, you!' We have a group hug and all pack up laughing.
As I walk into my house, the message tone on my phone rings – it's from Cole: *Drive safely 2nite njoy the party misin u already, luv u.*
My heart flutters, and I feel like a schoolgirl receiving her first love letter. After being together for such a long time, is it still possible to feel like this?
I text him back:
Will sleep ova at Denise's hse if I can't drive haha luv u so much c u early 2moro am.
First stop is Cheri's. She lives in a townhouse complex in Somerset West. I'm sure they could afford a bigger freestanding home, but Cheri prefers the security of a complex since Tian is away so much.
'So, are we ready for this?' She asks as she gets into my car.
I giggle, 'Not too sure what to expect really.'

'I am not stripping or getting involved in distasteful games! They can get mad at me if they like; I don't care.' She sticks out her bottom lip and her eyebrows furrow.

'Well, Cheri, as you said, we'll probably land up against the wall because I am not going to either, so we're in this together, okay?'

As she smiles, her good looks return.

We arrive at Sondra's house, which is only two blocks away from Cheri's. It's an old house that she rents from an uncle. On Monday, she is moving to Neville's house, so at the moment, there are boxes everywhere – organized chaos, or so she says. I hoot, Sondra comes out, locks the front door, and heads for the car. Before she's taken three steps, she turns around, unlocks the door again, disappears into the house, and comes back out, locking the door again, but this time with her handbag slung over her arm. She flops into the back seat and slams the car door.

'Sure you've got everything?' I say laughing.

'It has been absolute chaos here today! I've been trying to pack as much as I can, but I had to pop in at the florist and see the caterer. And I've had my mother around me all day, that is exhausting in itself – everything with her is wrong or an issue! I'm so tired now, I almost canceled tonight.' She sighs.

Cheri and I glance at each other. 'Well, then, a night out with us tonight is what you need!'

I pull off, and Cheri texts Denise to say that we'll be there in ten minutes.

'Seems it's busy tonight, hope we can get a decent seat.' I can see many moving shapes through the dimly lit windows, and it already looks full.

Walking into the club, one can't help but admire the way the entrance lounge is lit with low lighting, enhancing the paintings of celebrities along the walls. It is a Tudor-style building, with white walls and wooden beams crisscrossing the ceiling, well-maintained and sparkling clean. A door to the left leads us into the main entertainment lounge, a long and spacious area with a staging area at the far end where a band occasionally plays. There's a small dance floor in front of the stage, lit up with colored lights and a disco ball. The bar is to the right and takes up almost the entire length of the room. Neatly arranged tables and chairs fill the rest of the area.

We make our way to tables set up in a corner, where Denise and all the other ladies are waiting for us. Cheri and I both make sure we walk in front of Sondra as we approach.

Then Cheri and I part so that Denise can see Sondra, and before anyone else can join in, she yells 'SURPRISE' so loudly I think the whole world hears it.

Sondra lets out a loud screech, 'NO NO NOOO!' She doubles over with laughter and hides her face, not sure if she should be happy or embarrassed. In a flash, Denise rushes over and drags her off to the ladies' room. While we wait for them to come back, we introduce ourselves to the others and find a spot to sit near the wall on the left.

About ten minutes later, Denise and poor Sondra reappear – Sondra dressed up like a schoolgirl. I wonder how this evening will end up. Sondra's face goes every shade of red, and I think if a hole in the ground could swallow her up right now, she would gladly allow it to. Everyone cheers and whistles as she makes her entrance while a waiter pours Cheri and me a glass of red wine each. Denise has Sondra sit in a chair in the middle of the stage and gives a brief speech to thank everyone for being there. Then, everyone raises their glasses to Sondra's happiness; the lights go dim, and a seductive song begins to play over the speakers.

'Oh no, what are they going to make her do?' I look at Cheri, and she shrugs.

The words have barely left my tongue when a man appears on the stage. He is short but well-built, with dark hair smeared with body oil, and not particularly good-looking. He announces himself as 'Louie' and begins to prance around a humiliated Sondra in just a G-string and bowtie. As he nears her, he begins dancing more erotically. Almost on top of her, he starts rubbing himself up against her, trying to be as titillating as the screaming women encourage him to be. She covers her face with her hands and refuses to look at him until Glenda, the aunt Sondra has warned us about, ties her hands behind her back. The women are screaming, whistling, and shouting all kinds of obscenities at both Sondra and Louie the Stripper. Maybe there's something wrong with me because there is no way I am enjoying this or would ever even consider joining in. I look at Cheri, and she is looking down at her wine glass.

'Is this what we're supposed to be like, or am I just being a prude? Because I'm not enjoying this one bit!'

'Oh goodness, Tali, I can't stand this, it's so degrading!' Cheri exclaims vehemently, 'Why would anyone do this? Especially to someone you're supposed to like? If my bridesmaid did this to me, I would never speak to her again!'

I lean towards her, 'Well, she did warn us that she has a crazy family.'

Cheri leans back in her chair and plays with her hair. I lick my lips uncomfortably, wondering if I should do something to curb the situation. Now, Glenda is dancing with Louie and practically forcing him onto Sondra. The song ends, and Sondra gets up and begs another woman to untie her hands. She is obliged and gets up from the chair. The next song begins, and immediately, Louie starts dancing again. Sondra shakes her head, grabs Denise by the arm, and beckons to Louie. She says something in earnest to them, her hands wildly gesticulating as she tosses her head. Suddenly, Louie moves to the front of the stage, where, above the music, he thanks everyone for their time and leaves the room. From our spot in the corner, Cheri and I see Glenda staggering around, her eyes flashing as she starts ranting and raving. Before long, Denise and Glenda are in a full-fledged argument, their voices rising far above the deafening music. Sondra says something and turns on her heel, marching over to us.

'Please take me home,' she begs, tears in her voice, 'this is the worst day of my life!'

We hesitate. 'Crikey, Sondra! But won't there be an even bigger scene if you leave? They'll be so angry with you; they probably won't even come to the wedding!'

'Believe me, Tali,' Sondra looks at me in earnest, 'what you just saw is nothing. Glenda is blindingly drunk, and there's no stopping her when she's like this. It's what I feared; she won't relent until she's completely humiliated everyone here, and don't think she'll exclude you. Please let's go now before they notice!'

Cheri doesn't hesitate and immediately picks up her bag and motions to me with her hand. 'Let's go!'

We run on the left side of the room and out to the entrance, where the manager is standing.

'If they come looking for me, you haven't seen me, please!' Sondra looks at him beseechingly, 'I'm so sorry about this; if I'd known,' she glares and Cheri and me, 'I wouldn't have come.'

'It's okay, ma'am, don't you worry yourself, I'll sort them out soon enough.' He smiles kindly at her.

'Thanks, hey,' Sondra says in an angry tone of voice as we run out to the car.

I beep the car alarm, and in a few seconds, we're already halfway down the road.

'I'm so very, very sorry, Sondra! We didn't know this would happen! We were just told to get you here as a surprise! You know we would never have gone along with it if we'd known! I'm so sorry!' I feel like I cannot apologize to her enough.

Cheri nods fervently and repeats my explanation in an unusually high voice. Sondra sighs and leans back in her seat.

'Okay, sorry guys, thanks, at least, I know you weren't in on it. I know who is to blame, though, I'm just so grateful you agreed to leave. I felt like I wanted to die! How humiliating was that? How embarrassing? Glenda thinks that because she enjoys this kind of thing, everyone else will too. And you know what? If they don't come to the wedding, then that's just fine! Neville is going to be livid when he hears about this. Jeepers, I wish we were already married, so I wouldn't have to stress about what Glenda's going to get up to at the wedding. She is just impossible.' Sondra sniffs and reaches for her bag.

'Oh well, now we have the whole night ahead of us, so how about a movie?' Cheri suggests.

Ignoring Cheri, Sondra squeals, 'All my stuff is still there; my bag, my phone, and my clothes!'

I make a U-turn and head back to Shelter. As I enter, the manager notices me and approaches me immediately.

'Is there a problem, ma'am?' He asks.

'Is everyone still here? Oh gosh, I hope they aren't causing a scene, are they?' I looked around anxiously.

'No worries, ma'am, they're all entertaining themselves – we've set up karaoke for them!'

What a clever businessman.

'I've come back for Sondra's stuff, do you know if it is still in the ladies' room?'

'The waitress brought her things to me earlier; she was afraid they'd get forgotten in the bathroom. I've got everything in my office; I'll get it for you.' He strides off as I'm still asking him to thank the waitress.

Sondra changes her clothes rather awkwardly in the car while I'm driving. We giggle as she kicks the school shirt and pleated skirt under the seat. Eventually, we arrive at Somerset Mall. Sondra, still adjusting her jeans and T-shirt, lags behind as Cheri and I head for the ticket office. We decide to watch *The Bomber* with our favorite actor, Robert Dunbar, in it, and then head to The Café. There isn't enough time to have something to eat as well, so we have quick cappuccinos and, while we chat, decide we'll spend the night at my house and have a PJ party of our own.

'Here's to Sondra, a happy marriage, and our PJ party,' Cheri lifts her mug, and we join in, echoing, 'Here, here.'

We sip our drinks hurriedly, I pay the bill, and we run like little girls into the cinema.

After a great movie, we're back at my house, and I lend both of them a pair of my pajamas. We get comfy on the sofa bed with cups of Horlicks and chat away about Glenda, Denise, the movie, sexy Robert Dunbar, our partners, and Sondra's wedding. In the very wee hours of the morning, we all fell fast asleep.

A phone is vibrating on the table. I raise my head to make sure I'm not still dreaming, and realizing I'm not, nudge Sondra with my foot.

'Your phone, answer your phone.'

'Just a message, leave it,' she mumbles sleepily.

Two hours later, we stagger awake. I go straight to the kitchen and put the water on to boil. Sondra immediately checks her phone for messages, and Cheri rushes off to the bathroom.

'Message from Denise, she says she's sorry about last night and left about half an hour after we did.'

'You'd better tell Neville what happened before he finds out from someone else,' Cheri yells from the bathroom.

After coffee and showers, I drop everyone off and go straight to Cole's flat.

'So you survived the fearless Glenda, I hear,' Cole opens the door with a huge smile and envelops me in a bear hug. 'I missed you, love,' he says into my ear, kissing it lightly.

'Hey, it was just one night, and besides, you had such good company – a bunch of men together around a barbecue – what better way to spend a night?' I tease, 'I missed you too silly.' I kiss him softly and hold him.

Will I ever get tired of hugging and kissing him?

As I tell him about the evening with Glenda, Louie, and Robert Dunbar, Cole listens in fascination.

'Wow, you girls sure know how to entertain yourselves! Boy, is Neville going to have a fit, and now I know my competition is Robert, then, is it?' He grins and pokes me in the side.

'Oh goodness, love, I can't believe the way women go mad over strippers! I was so grateful when Sondra asked us to leave; it was awful!' I looked at my watch, 'Oops, we'd better go, or else we'll be late for lunch with your parents.'

His parents, Bob and Jeny, live in Durbanville, an hour's drive from here. Both retired but still very active; they're always traveling around the world. It's lovely to see how they always get so excited about their next trip. Cole is an only child and, until there are grandchildren, the world is theirs to explore. Well, that's how Bob justifies it anyway.

CHAPTER SEVEN

Sondra and Neville are to be wed at one o'clock on a smallholding in Hermanus, almost ninety kilometers away.

Knowing we are in for a gigantic feast, Cole and I stick to coffee and a few slices of toast with marmite and cheese for brunch. While we wait for the next slices of bread to toast, Cole licks the Marmite off the knife, repeatedly dipping it back into the bottle. I can only shake my head.

After a long, refreshing shower, I put on a knee-length dark green dress with three-quarter-length sleeves and a low V-neck with a broad waistband. I slip on a pair of black stilettos and grab a green and black pashmina to throw over my shoulders. As usual, I apply a hint of blush, mascara, and a brown-toned lipstick, and, for a change, I put on some eyeliner. I clip my hair back loosely with an emerald and onyx pin, leaving curls to frame my face. I finish myself off with a couple of good squirts of Chanel No. 5.

Satisfied that I look okay, I went to the lounge where Cole is balanced precariously on the couch, trying not to crease his suit. As my eyes come to rest on him, my heart skips a beat. He is so handsome and dashing.

Is this my Cole, sitting here in my house, wearing a beige-colored suit and a shirt that almost matches my dress?

He's not wearing a tie, but that doesn't matter – he looks perfect.

'Oh Cole, you're so beautiful!' I fight off the lump in my throat as I speak.

'Hey! That's supposed to be my line!' I notice him blush as he smiles his huge, beautiful smile and gets up to walk towards me. He takes my arms and holds them out straight, looks at me, and shakes his head.

'You, my love, are a vision.' Now it's my turn to blush.

He reaches into his jacket pocket and pulls out a little blue box. My heart starts beating wildly as he hands it to me.

'I saw these in Mossel Bay, and, well, I knew what color we were going to wear, so I thought they'd match well. I don't know if you'll like them, though…'
He sounds so adorable, so sheepish and unsure; it's not often that he buys me gifts.
I loudly exclaim as I eagerly open the little box 'Oh love, they're so beautiful! They're so perfect, this is, um, this is, just so perfect, they're so beautiful!'
I am a little lost for words. What a beautiful pair of earrings – an emerald stone set in white gold in an upside-down teardrop; just long enough so that the stone will hang below my earlobe.
'I'll just go and put them on,' and hurry to the mirror in my room.
Looking at my reflection, I cannot help but believe nothing could've matched more perfectly. The earrings, along with the color of my dress, transformed my pale green eyes to a rich, almost emerald green, as though I were wearing colored contact lenses.
Cole walks into the room and looks at me, still afraid I might not like them.
'Do you like them?'
'I love them; I love you, they're perfect, you're perfect, thank you so much, I can't believe you did this, you're so sneaky!' I splutter, smiling and giggling at the same time; eventually, we're ready to go.
The drive along the coast to Hermanus is spectacularly beautiful. There was a slight breeze in the air, and the sun bright and warm. The road felt smooth in Cole's 4x4, unlike how it would have felt in my little car. To pass the time, we took bets on what style and color Sondra's dress would be, whether the men would wear tuxedos, and even on the style and type of flowers in the bouquet. I know I'll win that one, thanks to Sondra, who wouldn't stop talking about her florist at work. Suddenly, my heart sinks as I remember Josh will be in our company all day.
'Argh, I just remembered Josh is going to be there. What are we going to say to him for practically a whole day? I don't even know what his interests are!' I groan.

'Well, guess we'll find out soon enough. At least it's not only us at the table. Maybe he and Tian will hit it off well, and we won't have to worry about him at all!'
'Oh, I like the way you think, but Cheri won't be happy about that. I still can't get over the fact that he's going to be there. It just doesn't make sense at all!'

Arriving at the venue, we are both in awe of the beauty surrounding us; it's as though God painted the place just for the wedding – blue mountains to our left and a turquoise sea to our right. The leaves on the trees are autumn colors, presenting a stunning contrast to the dazzling blue hues around us. The grass is bright green, and the lawn is cut so smoothly it looks artificial.

We walk down a gravel pathway towards a quaint chapel, still with its original walls and floor, and small stained-glass windows. The only new feature is a thatch roof. Enveloping the chapel are large bushes of lavender, and as the breeze blows across my face, I get a whiff of their rich scent. Behind the chapel is a large marquee tent, where the reception will be held. In the garden to the right of the chapel are wrought iron chairs and a table with Sherry and cranberry juice for the guests, and while sipping our drinks, we admire the most incredible view of the sea.

'Oh, this is just too stunning! What a beautiful place and the view of the sea is out of this world!' I stand, amazed, wishing I could lie down on the lawn and absorb the view for hours, never to forget it.

'Wow, this is something else! There are no words to describe it!' Cole, like me, is trying to take it all in, to absorb the beauty to take home with us.

Cheri and Tian arrive and join us for a glass of sherry. We stand in silence, as though if we speak, this perfect painting will crack and disintegrate.

The guests arrive slowly and congregate in the garden with refreshments, greeting one another with hugs and smiles. Most, however, are doing just what we are doing, admiring the spectacular view in silence. A deep voice behind us startles us from our dream-like states, 'Hello, Tali, Cheri.'

We gather ourselves and look at him approvingly as he continues to speak, 'Hello, I'm Josh De Luca,' he says, and shakes Cole and Tian's hands. 'Hello Josh, this is Cole, my boyfriend, and Cheri's husband Tian,' I recover quickly and introduce the men to him.

'Wow, if I weren't married and he wasn't my boss...' Cheri whispers in my ear.

I smile, wanting to burst out laughing because it's what I'm thinking too. 'Isn't this place beautiful?' I say to distract myself.

'It is. I came here once before for a fortieth anniversary celebration; I couldn't get enough of the beauty then, and it's the same now. The mountains seemed greener then, though maybe because it was an overcast day.' Josh looks around in admiration. *I'm sure there isn't a place on this earth he hasn't been to;* I think cattily.

Josh is wearing a black, double-breasted suit, likely from Armani or another expensive brand, a light blue shirt, and a black tie. No matter how dashing Cole and Tian look, he outshines them both.

A man rings a bell and requests that we all take our places in the chapel. It's dark and cold inside, with pews on either side of the aisle leading up towards an altar at the front. Two steps, the width of the chapel, lead up to the altar, and on either side, there are huge flower arrangements mostly made up of shades of blue. As cold and dark as the chapel may be, it has a warm and peaceful atmosphere.

Neville and his best man are sitting in the front pew to the right, both looking very smashing in their black tuxedos. As he looks around and sees us enter, he waves and smiles nervously. We make our way to seats in the middle of the pews on the left; Cheri first, then Tian, Josh, me, and then Cole. I lean over and motion for Cheri to move next to me. She shrugs her shoulders and looks annoyed.

'Cheri, please swap places with me, and then you and Tali can compare notes during the ceremony.' Josh must have been watching me.

Josh laughs at his joke, and Cole snickers too.
'Thanks so much, that's very thoughtful of you,' Cheri says, as the three of them play musical chairs.
I feel my cheeks flush and wish I could sink into the floor as Cheri sits down next to me and nudges me in the ribs, giggling.
'This is going to be an interesting day, isn't it?'

We're asked to rise as two pretty little girls enter. They are wearing light blue dresses and ballet shoes, each carrying a basket of rose petals that they scatter on the ground as they walk up the aisle. Then Denise enters the chapel. Her dress is the same shade of blue as the flower girls', but it is long and silky, and she wears matching blue sandals. At last, Sondra makes her entrance on her father's arm. She looks too beautiful, radiant in a champagne-colored dress embroidered with lace and pearls. The back of her dress flows into a long train that trails along the floor behind her as she walks. She is not wearing a veil so that we can see her hair, up-styled with delicate white flowers scattered among the curls. Her makeup is very natural, and she is wearing small pearl earrings and a matching pearl choker around her neck.
'She is perfect,' Cheri whispers to me.
I nod my head and smile, noticing a grin on everyone's faces, even Josh's.

The ceremony is simple and short. Neville battles to get his 'I do's' out; he is so nervous, which makes us all laugh. Once the ceremony is over, the couple signs the register, and we make our way outside to wait, armed with rose petals to throw over them as they exit the chapel.

Covered with rose petals, Sondra, Neville, and the rest of the bridal party disappear to have photos taken, and we all head to the reception marquee to find our table. Cheri and I make sure to sit next to each other straight away. Josh sits down next to Cole.
'Can I pour everyone a glass of wine?' Josh rises and picks up a bottle of red wine from the table.

We chorus, 'Yes, thank you,' and he pours generously for each of us.

There is a screech of laughter from the marquee entrance, and as we all turned around, we see it's Glenda making her way to her table – a bottle of wine in her left hand and a full glass in her right.

'Oh goodness, the party hasn't even started. I hope she doesn't embarrass Sondra,' I look worriedly at Cheri.

'I think Neville will knock her block off her shoulders, after the hen party episode, if she causes any more trouble tonight!'

'Who is that?' Josh asks curiously, motioning in Glenda's direction.

'That's Glenda, Sondra's crazy aunt,' I explained what happened at the hen party and how we thought she'd be so angry she wouldn't come to the wedding. As it turned out, she couldn't remember a thing the next day; she had gotten so blitzed. That Josh should be witness to such a person makes it hard not to feel embarrassed for Sondra's sake.

'Oh well, we all have at least one such person in our families, in some form or manner,' he shrugs.

I laugh and say, 'That we do,' and take a sip of my wine.

Cheri giggles and also sips her wine.

Is this going to be a long night? I wonder.

'Have you known Sondra for long or just since working at Rio?' Josh looks at both Cheri and me as he asks.

'No, just since work; the three of us have become good friends.' Cheri smiles fondly.

He turns to Cole and asks, 'And what work do you do?'

Cole tells him in brief, and I listen while Josh asks several questions, seeming genuinely interested in Cole's line of work.

While they are discussing Cole's vocation, Tian and Cheri join in the conversation, and it's not long before everyone knows everything about everyone else's job.

We learn how De Luca came to South Africa from Italy, chasing after a woman he met while she was on holiday in Italy. He found her, married her, and has lived here ever since. Josh went to university and then lived in Italy for a year. In the meantime, De Luca founded Rio Adventures as international tourism in South Africa began to take significant strides. Eventually, Josh made his way back to South Africa and joined the business. It's interesting listening to him telling De Luca's story. Suddenly, Josh becomes a human being, not just a body without a character, who walks around the office all day.

Then the bridal party enters the marquee, and we all stand and clap as they make their way to the bridal table. They go straight into the speeches – first, Neville's best man has us in hysterics, and then Neville has us all in tears.

Meals get served, and the men are delighted to discover they can have as many helpings as they wish. Why is it that weddings always seem to make the men have more of an appetite than usual?

After dinner, Sondra and Neville take to the floor for their first dance, and an Afrikaans song that none of us know accompanies them. I am pleasantly surprised at how good a dancer Sondra is, and Neville looks good thanks to her! The two sets of parents, Denise and the best man, join them on the dance floor, and then everyone else is invited to join in. I know Cole won't want to dance just yet, so I sit back and watch.
After a few dances, the cake is cut, the flowers and garter thrown, and then it's just time to enjoy the celebration.

I cringe as I notice Glenda walking to our table. Before Cheri or I can escape, she introduces herself at the top of her voice to the men.
'What a handsome table! I should be sitting here; I will be the rose amongst the thorns. So which one of you delicious young men is going to ask me to dance?' She slurs and saliva spurts from her mouth. She sways in a figure 8 motion, grabbing hold of the back of the unoccupied chair seconds before she falls over.
'Glenda, someone is calling you over there!' I point to the other end of the tent.
She spins around, almost taking the chair with her, and starts stumbling that way, and then changes direction and heads for

the dance floor, where she begins to dance with her glass of wine. A young boy takes the glass from her, and it looks as though he is going to dance with her, then suddenly he walks away. Glenda carries on by herself, swaying to and fro with the beat. While we watch her, Tian thanks me for orchestrating the escape, pulling a face when he says how he could smell the alcohol on her breath.

The DJ plays a lively song that has everyone on their feet. Cole is not the greatest of dancers, but he can enjoy himself, especially to this type of music. When it comes to classical dances like the waltz or slower dances, he heads for his chair very quickly.

My parents are great dancers; we used to have our own private parties, just my dad, mum, Eric, and me, dancing the night away. We learned the waltz, the foxtrot, the jive, to name but a few. Eric would always say how being able to dance is a great chick magnet, and it horrified my mother every time.

We are all laughing and dancing away when I look at our table and realize that Josh is still sitting there alone.
'Oh dear, he's all by himself. He really should've brought a partner along!' I feel bad.
'Well, you'll just have to dance with him then, won't you?' Cole's eyes twinkle.
'Forget it, don't you dare do that to me!'
Cole laughs, enjoying my discomfort. When the song comes to an end all too soon, the DJ takes a break, and we all go back to our tables.
'Do you enjoy dancing at all, Josh?' Cole asks him.
He wouldn't dare, would he?
'Actually, I do very much. I can dance fairly well; my aunt, with whom I lived in Italy, is an instructor, and she taught me.'
'Well then, when the DJ plays a waltz or that type of music, you can take Tali for a turn on the floor, she's good herself.'
I kick his leg under the table and glare at him. I cannot believe he is doing this to me. He knows how I feel about Josh and is

so cruelly amused by my agitation. I am not at all impressed. Cheri almost chokes on her wine when she hears Cole's offer.

'Well, Tali, I would enjoy that very much, if you would oblige me?' Josh politely turns to me.

'Sure.'

What else am I supposed to say? No, I don't want to?

Cole knows I would never do that. I kick him again and pinch his leg until he flinches. Good! I hope he feels the pain.

It is not much longer before the DJ decides to play slower music and, as expected, Josh asks me to dance.

We make our way onto the dance floor, where he holds me in a perfect pose, the correct distance apart, and we begin to glide across the floor. He dances incredibly well, so gracefully that I can hardly feel my feet on the floor. After a while, I feel as though everyone is watching us. They aren't, of course, as we aren't the only people on the dance floor, but it feels like it. The first song ends far too quickly, but another one starts, and off we go again. I'm enjoying myself, and now and again I catch Cole smiling in approval as we swirl past. He knows how much fun I am having, so he enjoys watching.

'Where did you learn to dance?' Josh asks as we dance, and I tell him about my parents and our private parties.

'Must have been so much fun, not many parents do things like that anymore. I like your father.'

'You know my dad?' I ask, surprised, and it shows.

'Yes, you know we do business with his company from time to time. I always talk to him whenever I get the chance.'

'Oh yes, sorry, I forgot about that. Yes, he is a wonderful person.' I do not let the conversation go on any further. I prefer that he not be familiar with my personal life. We continue dancing for three more songs and then return to the table. I'm rather tired and sip my wine.

'Tali dances well, thank you for sparing her, Cole.' Josh sits down and smiles at me.

'You're welcome. It's always lovely to dance with someone who knows what they're doing.' I reply before Cole can, smiling sweetly at Josh.

Cole, of course, just laughs at me.

In the car on our way home, I punch Cole playfully on the arm.
'How could you do that to me? Make me dance with Josh like that? You found it very amusing, didn't you?'
'Do you have any idea how great it was to watch you dance like that? I know you love it, and with me, you don't get the chance; you looked like a pro!'
'He's very good, so I won't take all the credit for looking good. But yes, I did enjoy it. Suppose I must thank you now?'
'Oh, you can thank me at home,' Cole grins mischievously.

CHAPTER EIGHT

The day of our staff meeting finally arrives. The meetings are never long, though, thank goodness. De Luca gets on with business quickly and efficiently. He says there's no time for messing around, but always allows us to raise any opinions, objections, or related work points. He will debate an issue and either resolve it or make a point of resolving it as expeditiously as possible, and he always keeps his promises.

Sondra, Cheri, and I make our way to the boardroom on the fourth floor. There is a large table in the center of the room that seats at least 20 people. As with the rest of the building, the room is very light and airy due to its large windows and the half-open blinds. As always, we head for the seats nearest the windows at the end of the table, as far away from De Luca as possible. We make sure we arrive first to secure these seats. Greg and Brett, being the lazy men that they are, always arrive last, and the result is that they get the seats closest to De Luca. It doesn't bother them, though, frankly, nothing does.

De Luca arrives, sits down as he greets everyone and gets on with business. There is not much to discuss today aside from the team-building event that needs to be arranged. It's agreed that we will go on a hike up Table Mountain and then abseil down. Cheri is silently horrified, but Sondra and I are elated. In our books, the abseiling is going to be so much fun. Josh confirms the date for next month, the weekend of July 15th, and I cannot wait to tell Cole; he is going to be so jealous. We are all excitedly talking about it when Josh clears his throat and says he wants to raise something.

'A little matter not noted on the agenda, but I want to get everyone's opinion,' he clears his throat again.

We all hush to listen to what he has to say.

'I was in the elevator the other day, and the person I was with suggested we put cartoons on the doors, so it's not so boring or silent on the ride up. To make things a little lighter and more jovial here, you know?'

I want to die. I wish the floor would open up and swallow me. I can feel my face flush. Sondra and Cheri start snickering.

Why did he take me seriously?

Surprisingly enough, everyone thinks it's a great idea, and it's decided that Greg and Brett will get onto it right away. The cartoons will get changed every four months. It will run for a year, and then the entire project will get re-evaluated. I have no opinion at all, and for the rest of the meeting, I sit in silence, Sondra and Cheri continuously giggling at my rather obvious discomfort.

Walking out of the boardroom, I catch Josh looking at me with a huge smile on his face. All I can do is shake my head and grin back sheepishly.

In the office, Sondra and Cheri don't stop laughing at me, but I have to admit it will be very interesting to see what the outcome of the first cartoons is.

While I check my emails, I find one from Josh:

Hello Tali, I told you it wasn't a bad idea. Josh.

I blurt it out to Sondra and Cheri, who look at me in astonishment.

Lately, Josh has become more of a human being than we've ever known him to be.

'Are you going to reply?' Cheri asks.

'What am I supposed to say?'

'Just say you're pleased you could be of assistance?'

That's what I do*:*

So glad I could be of assistance, Tali.

'What did you get from him as a wedding present, by the way?' I ask Sondra curiously, remembering how she and Neville joked about only inviting him for the gift he would give.

'Oh, he gave us R1000.00, not bad at all, I would say.'

'Not bad, wow, that's impressive! No wonder you let him stay!'

Cheri chips in, 'Did you see him take Tali around the dance floor? They looked just like professionals!'

'Oh, stop it, it wasn't that great!' I flush again. 'I mean, he dances brilliantly, so he just made me look good. I must say, though, it was wonderful to dance with him…'
'Oh, I saw that all right! Everyone did! Everyone couldn't stop saying what a wonderful couple you made and how you danced together like a dream!' Sondra replies teasingly.
'They did not!' I retort very quickly.
'Well, you two looked great dancing together, and there's no denying it, Tali,' Cheri is adamant.
I keep quiet in the hope that they will drop the subject.

I phone Cole and get his voicemail; he's probably in an interview, so I leave him a rather smug message about the upcoming teambuilding event. Cole, of course, has done abseiling before and loved it. I also mentioned that I have something else to tell him. I know he will be very curious for the rest of the day, and before long, I get a text:
You get fired. What happened? Will c u later, got to go back to interview now, luv u.
I chuckle to myself as I sip my coffee.

CHAPTER NINE

I make myself comfortable on Cole's couch. The local newspaper never holds my interest for long, so within minutes I've finished paging through it. I cuddle up and shut my eyes for a moment. It's no more than half an hour when Cole arrives, sits next to me, and shakes my arm gently.

'Hey, sleepy, wake up, you've got something to tell me,' I look up, and his beautiful face is smiling down at me.

I have to laugh as I know he's been curious all day. You can't keep anything from him; he just won't let you.

'Remember the day I mentioned to Josh about putting cartoons on the elevator doors?' Cole nods, 'Well, he decided to mention it in the staff meeting and asked everyone's opinion, and everyone thought it was a great idea! So Greg and Brett have been put to the task. I thought Cheri and Sondra were going to die laughing!'

'Wow, do you get to have the final say, since it was your idea?'

'Oh no, no one knows it was my idea, and it's going to stay that way, that's for sure. So, how was your interview?'

'Oh, it was amazing. He's an ex-Navy admiral who dedicates all his free time to coaching children with disabilities in wheelchair baseball. What an incredible man! Been to every inch of this earth and has seen so much, and out of all the places in the world to spend his last days, he's settled on Fish Hoek. He told me such inspiring stories about the kids and how, through wheelchair baseball, they've found direction in life. He knows that other guy I interviewed, Nick Drummond. Do you remember him? I told you about him.'

'Yes, the, um, horse commentator.'

'Yes, clever girl. Well, they work for the same charities and attend the same church. He said that Nick mentioned me to him. Told him what a good chap I am. So, when he heard it was me coming to do the interview, he was pleased, as I came highly recommended.' Cole grins and rubs his chest with his fingers as if shining a badge.

I smile at him, and I can clearly see how thrilled and proud he is at having made such an impression.

'What's his name?'

'Henry Lategan. He is eighty-six years old, and all the years in the sun haven't done much damage – he looks much younger than he is. He still walks on the beach almost every day; he says you should take the time to absorb the earth you live on, and you will find peace. He's such a great man.'

Cole stands up, walks to the kitchen, opens the fridge, and stares at the contents as though the food is going to jump out at him and beg to be made into dinner. Sighing, he suggests we go to Rumps for our favorite steaks. Naturally, I agree, and yet I feel as though there is something else he wants to tell me.

Rump is as busy as usual. We settle into the lounge and enjoy a glass of wine while we wait for a table. The owners, as always, make time to come and chat with us, and it's not very long before we are seated and place our orders. Cole cannot stop fidgeting with the cutlery, and I just have to ask him what's going on.

Pausing for a short moment, but not long enough for him to answer me, I continue, 'It seems like you want to talk about something, but you don't know how to.'

While I hold his hand, he looks down at mine and plays with the ring on my forefinger. Then he smiles and looks at me, as though relieved that I've picked up on it.

'My, you are very perceptive,' he takes a sip of wine, 'you know that man I was telling you about earlier?' He does not wait for my reply. 'Well, he also spoke to me about God, as Nick Drummond did. Like Nick, he said I should think about it, so I said I would. Then on the way home, I did and remember I said if I wanted anyone to study with me, it would be you and your dad,' he pauses, 'well, would you?' He stares at me, his eyes seeking mine for an answer. He knows what my answer will be, but he still looks for one; this is not what I expected at all, and for some reason, I feel I need to confirm that I've heard correctly.

'You want us to study the Gospel with you?'

'Yes, please, but if you don't want to, it's okay.'
'Don't want to? Why wouldn't I want to? Cole, this is wonderful; I'm so happy.' Oblivious of the other people in the restaurant, I exclaim loudly and stretch across the table to hug him. 'I'm really happy, my love. I know I haven't been the best example of a Christian. I've lost my way a lot, and I think studying with you will help me too. Oh boy, I do hope you're ready for my mum, she's going to explode with happiness!' I giggle, 'Thank you for asking me; I love you so much.' I kiss him lightly.
He holds my hand and kisses it tenderly. The moment gets duly ruined with the arrival of our food.
I get my cell phone out of my bag and dial my dad's number.
'When do you want to start?' I ask him quickly before my father answers.
'Hello Talia-May, this is a lovely surprise!' I smile when I hear his gruff voice.
'Hi, Daddy, it's not a bad time, is it?' I'm not sure if he's in a study group or some other meeting.
'No, no, still got a few minutes before we begin, is something the matter?' He suddenly sounds concerned.
'Um, do you want to ask him?' I quickly ask Cole, afraid of rushing him.
He shakes his head and gestures for me to continue.
'No, Dad, nothing's wrong, but I have got some great news,' I pause to add some dramatic suspense to my exciting news, 'Dad, Cole wants to study with you and me. He wants to learn the Gospel.'
I smile at Cole and speak excitedly at the same time.
'Oh! Praise the Lord, this is wonderful!' My dad exclaims on the other end.
'When will it suit you? It will probably be best at your place?'
'Well, you're coming over on Thursday as always, so we can start then. May I speak to him, please?'
I give my cell phone to Cole without replying.
Cole looks a little nervous when he speaks, 'Um, good evening, Leon, how are you?'
'Ah, Cole, my boy, I'm very well and delighted; this is a good thing you are doing; you will see. I told Talia-May that we can

start on Thursday since you're going to be at our place for dinner, will that be okay with you?'

'Yeah, that makes sense. Tali can fill me in on anything that I need to bring along.'

'I have everything you will need; you just bring an open heart that's willing to hear - this makes me very happy, Cole. Talia-May's mum and I have been praying for this for a long time now. But I won't scare you off just yet, so we'll see you on Thursday then.'

He says goodbye to me as well, tells me once more how happy he is, and then hangs up.

I put the phone down, squeeze Cole's hand, and giggle excitedly. By the time we start eating our steaks, they're cold, but we don't mind.

On our way home, my cell phone rings, 'My mum. You want to answer it?'

I know she will want to talk to Cole, so I hand him the phone. 'Hello, Rose.'

I can hear her talking nonstop, her voice escalating with every word. All Cole can get in is "thank you," "yes," and finally "goodbye."

'Wow, she is excited,' he says, returning the phone to me. 'What do you think Eric will say?'

'Oh, he'll be happy all right. I wonder if Judith will be encouraged by you. Maybe she isn't even aware that Eric is a Christian. Wow, that's shocking; thinking about it now, both Eric and I have adopted a very lazy attitude towards our Christianity. I will have to study with you to get back on track.'

Cole does not seem to be listening. He is far away in thought, and for a moment I feel a wave of panic wash over me – maybe I've rushed things.

'Cole, Thursday is okay, isn't it? It isn't too soon for you?'

He looks at me a bit confused, 'Why do you ask that?'

'I don't know, just for a minute, I thought I might have rushed things. Normally, when people ask to study, it's weeks before the first lesson takes place.'

'Well, no, not at all. I think if I wanted to wait weeks, I wouldn't have asked you now. Thursday is good, love,' he pats my leg and smiles at me.

We reach my house.

'Just one thing, though,' Cole says as we walk into the house, 'don't say anything to my parents just yet, they'll have so many questions, and I'd rather wait until we finish the study, so I have decent and correct answers for them. The other thing is that, um, I don't have a Bible.'

He grimaces as though I will think badly of him for not having one. I hug him tightly. He is simply the kindest and sweetest person on earth.

'Not to worry, my dad has plenty.'

We make Horlicks, and while Cole is in the shower, I sit up in bed and, for the first time in a very long time, I pray with an earnest and sincere heart. My prayer has a genuine feeling and meaning, and it comes from the depths of my heart. For a long time, my prayers have just been words. Cole's decision tonight has made me realize what a lazy, lukewarm Christian I have become, and I decide that this will have to change.

CHAPTER TEN

It's Thursday today, which means dinner with my parents and our first study with Cole. I know that dinner tonight will be very different – for one, my mum is going to prepare even more of a feast than usual.

I'm at the office before the others, so I put the coffee machine on and open the blinds. For a few minutes, as has become a habit, I stare out of the window. It is still very dark outside; winter is here.

'Hello, ladies,' I say as I hear them come in, 'cup of coffee?'

'My stupid car wouldn't start this morning, so luckily Cheri hadn't left yet when I called her,' is Sondra's reply.

'Well, can I brighten up your day with some good news?' I ask as I hand them their steaming cups of coffee. I have to tell them; I have to share this good news.

They both call themselves "Sunday Morning Christians," they go to church on Sundays, and that's where their Christianity ends. More than what I have been in the last few years, at least!

'Cole proposed?' This is Sondra's response to any bit of good news I bring to the table.

'No, silly, you do want that to happen, hey? Cole asked if he could study with my dad last night.'

They are silent, and at least half a minute passes before they respond.

'That's a surprise. What brought this about?' Cheri responds first.

I chuckle, 'Close your mouth, Sondra! We were at Rumps last night, and he came out with it. He did an interview with this man, and they got talking, like what happened with that Nick Drummond man and, well, I guess something must have hit home. So, we're going to start studying with my dad tonight.'

'That is wonderful, Tali; you've often said you need to go back, so this will help you too.'

'Exactly,' the phone on my desk rings. 'Who wants to bet that's my mum?' I walk to my desk and pick up the phone.

'Talia-May, it's your mum,' I give Sondra and Cheri a thumbs up and laugh silently. They smile, go to their respective desks, and sit down to get going with the day's work.

'Hello Mum, it's Thursday, I know, we will be there for dinner tonight, don't worry.'

'Oh, Talia-May, I'm so excited for tonight. I'm going to make a special dinner. Have you told Eric yet?'

'Mum, please don't worry about making a huge dinner; something light would be better. At least, then we can stay awake to study – if we're too full, we won't be able to. I haven't told Eric yet, Mum; I'll do so tonight.'

'Hmmm, maybe you're right about the food. Well, I will still make a decent meal, and then we can have snacks while studying. I won't say anything to Eric until you do, but it's going to be hard to contain my excitement when I speak to him just now.'

'Mum, please try to contain your excitement tonight, I don't want to scare Cole off before he even starts studying.'

'Oh, Talia-May! Of course, I will behave myself, I'm not stupid, you know.'

'I didn't say you were Mum. Anyway, we will see you later; do you want me to bring anything?'

'Of course not, I love you, see you tonight.'

And as always, she hangs up before I can say goodbye. She probably started dialing Eric's number before she even put the receiver down.

I smile and shake my head, and as I start pulling papers out of my in-tray that need attending to, my phone rings again. It's Brett.

'We've been told you can help us with the cartoon on the elevator?'

'Who told you that?' I'm not amused. I had hoped my name would get kept out of this.

'Josh suggested it. He seems to think you'll have some great ideas. We didn't know you two were buddies?'

'We are not!' It comes out too loudly and too quickly.

Sondra and Cheri look up at me curiously.

I put the phone down and scowl, 'Suddenly, Josh is all 'Mr. Friendly – what is wrong with him?'

I leave the office in a huff, not in the mood for either Brett or Greg today, and if Josh is there, I will certainly not be impressed. Walking into the elevator, I stare at the doors, picturing them covered in cartoons. I can't help but laugh at myself.

'Well, you sure got yourself into this one,' I sigh.

'Morning, Suzie,' I say as I walk past her desk. She's on the phone, so she waves at me as I head for Brett's office.

'Hey Tali, here are a few suggestions, what do you think?' Greg looks at me expectantly.

I'm quite impressed. There are five different cartoons, all very funny and excellently sketched. We eventually decide on one that includes Booker and June. We are sure she won't mind, but I suggest they run it by her first. It's all about June getting the Overlanders ready for a tour and Booker trying to help her. I think they should take everything to Josh for approval, but the one with Booker and June will get my vote.

At lunchtime, I make my way to a Christian bookshop wanting to buy something for Cole. I know my dad will give him a Bible, so I decide on a Bible case – one that zips closed and has pockets for a notebook and pen. It's leather, and for an extra R80.00, they will engrave his name, Cole Mellors, on it. I know he'll like it.

Eric and Judith are already at my parents' house when I get there. Cole hasn't arrived yet, which I am grateful for, as now I can tell them about him.

As always, Jack is first to greet me. I bend down and pat him, then walk into the kitchen, where Eric, Judith, my mum, and dad are chatting. Mum has an enormous smile on her face and is clearly bursting to tell Eric and Judith the good news. My dad is his normal, calm self, but I can see a little twinkle in his eyes.

'So, Mum tells us you have some good news?' Eric says in anticipation.

'Yeah, excellent news,' I reply, dragging the news out a bit longer.

'Oh, Talia-May, don't tease, tell him, or I'll tell him!' My mum can't contain herself for much longer.

'You most certainly will not!' I glare at my mum and then turn to Eric, 'Cole has asked dad to study with him; he wants to hear the Good News.''

I'm not sure how Eric will respond because I'm pretty sure he's become as lukewarm a Christian as I have.

'This is great news, Tali, great news, wow, and a surprise too! What made him decide to study?'

They intently listen as I tell them about the interviews with Nick Drummond and Henry Lategan.

'Wow, we never do think of these great sportspersons as Christians,' Judith says for the first time in the conversation.

I'm surprised by her comment and still unsure whether she's a Christian.

'Are you a Christian?' I ask her, maybe a little too bluntly, but it's out before I know it.

'I'm not sure, I went to church with my parents on Sundays, but that was it. I've never thought about it more than that, and Eric and I haven't discussed it.'

I immediately see the disapproval on my mum's face, although no one else does.

'Well, you're welcome to join us, if you would like to,' my dad offers.

Before Judith can reply, Jack goes hysterical, and Cole walks into the house. I go over to him and give him a huge hug, and, of course, my mum is right on my heels.

'Oh, Cole, I'm so happy you're taking this step.' She flushes with joy.

Cole hugs her back, 'Thanks, Rose.'

'Good move, Cole,' Eric says and shakes Cole's hand.

'Good evening, Leon, thanks for doing this for me,' Cole says, shaking my dad's hand with perfect manners as always.

'Goodness me, it's all my pleasure, son.'

I can hear the happiness in my dad's voice.

All of us are standing in the kitchen talking about how our day was when Mum announces that dinner is ready. As always, it's a feast fit for a king; so much for our discussion on the phone this morning! On the table are mixed carrots, peas, and corn; mashed potatoes with gravy and a variety of sausages: pork, boerewors, Russians, and Frankfurters.

We sit at the table for a while, waiting as the overindulgence of our food intake subsides. Once our muscles allow us to move, we make our way to the lounge. Eric and Judith excuse themselves, so Mum and Dad sit on the armchairs, and Cole and I sit on the couch. Suddenly, my mum gets up again and disappears into her bedroom for a few seconds. She returns, holding a Bible for Cole, with a little message of encouragement written on the inside and already placed in the leather cover I had bought.
'Wow, thanks so much, Rose and Leon!' Cole is touched. 'I told Tali I've never had one, and she said you would have one for me. I never realized it would be such a fancy one, though. Thank you very much.'
It's easy to see how sincere he is, as he stares at the Bible cover for a little while.
'You are so very welcome! It's a study Bible with lots of guidelines for every verse and chapter, and it also gives you a bit of history at the beginning of every book,' my dad explains as he shows Cole his own Bible.
'Well, shall we get started then? Let's pray,' he says as we bow our heads and take hands.

Just before midnight, we leave the house. The study went well; Cole asked questions freely, and my dad had all the answers, justifying everything with scripture. Cole seems to be grasping the truth of the death, burial, and resurrection quicker than I thought he would, and we are going to continue next Thursday again.

Cole goes home to his flat as he has to leave at 05:00 to catch a flight to Durban for another interview.

When I'm almost home, my cell phone, lying on the seat next to my leg, rings, and I put it on speaker.

'Hi, you home yet?'

'Just about to pull in. You?'

I click the remote to open the garage door and drive in.

'Almost, just wanted to make sure you're safe and sound. Thanks for tonight. I can't believe how simple and natural it is. What a fool I've been to have waited so long!'

'It happens to most of us. I'm really happy you're doing this, Cole.'

'Do you think we can carry on before Thursday?' Cole asks pleadingly.

'I'm sure it won't be a problem. I will check with my dad; maybe tomorrow night, if you like? I'm not sure what days he has what on.'

'Okay, great, thanks for this, hey, I'll speak to you tomorrow. Sleep tight, and I love you.'

'Okay, chat tomorrow, love you too.'

Oh my goodness, it's cold! I hug my duvet and, just for a second, I contemplate calling in sick. I know, without even opening my blinds, that it is going to be a freezing, very wet day. The second thought to enter my fuzzy mind is whether Booker will have set the controlled temperature in the building. I even go so far as to wonder if I have his cell phone number so I can remind him! Today has to be the coldest day of the year by far. My next thought is how long we still have to wait until summer.

Eventually, I drag myself out of bed and get ready for work. As I leave home, I feel a bit like an Eskimo – bundled up in boots, jeans, stockings, socks, a jersey, a thick jacket, a woolen cap, and a scarf. I know the jacket, scarf, and cap will come off in the office, but my little car's heater doesn't work so well. Even if it is just a short drive to the office, my objective is to be warm at all times.

On my way, I call my dad, hoping to catch him before he leaves for the office.
'Hi Dad, how are you?'
'Good morning, Talia-May, this is a pleasant surprise so early in the morning.'
'Yeah, I wanted to catch you before you get too involved in your day. Cole wants to carry on with the study before Thursday; will you be able to fit him in at all?'
'That's wonderful to hear; we can continue tonight if you like? It's Friday, and there is no need for me to be at the youth meeting, so tonight would be good.'
'Thanks, Dad, he's in Durban today, so I'll speak to him when he phones me, but otherwise, we will see you after work. Thanks again, Dad, this is helping me a lot too.'
'Always here for you, my love.'
'Bye, Dad, see you later. I love you.'

I end the call, then see a message on my phone. It is from Cole, reminding me to phone my dad. He says he'll see me tonight and, of course, that he loves me. I just smile. He's perfect for me and now even more so.

Booker stands at the door as always.
'Morning, Miss Medeck, lovely weather we're having.'
I glare at him, 'You are joking, aren't you?'
'Oh no, this is the best time of the year.'
'Booker, please tell me you've set the building temperature to a lot warmer than this?'
Booker laughs at my discomfort. I think my lips are turning blue already.
'Of course, I did, Miss Medeck; I wouldn't want to have everyone unhappy. I will just stand outside to enjoy this lovely weather.'
'Booker, there must be something wrong with you, but thank you very much. I will be much happier in my warm office than out here.'
I hug him. He is such a happy person and always so considerate.

My office is already at room temperature. Taking off my jacket, cap, and scarf as I knew I would, I put the coffee machine and radio on, and am opening the blinds as Sondra and Cheri walk in. They are also complaining about the cold and are very grateful for the warmth in the office. We stand together at the window and look out at the rain, wishing summer were here so we could complain about the heat.
'Cole had his first study last night,' I say excitedly, 'we were going to carry on next Thursday, but he asked to carry on tonight. He is enjoying it.'
'Who would've thought?' Cheri responds.
They both know how I grew up in the church and have often asked why I fell away. They always get the same answer – that I don't know why, it just happened over a long period, even before I met Cole.
'Maybe you will start going to church on Sundays now? Your mum will be over the moon. I can see her introducing you to

everyone like a peacock showing off its feathers!' Sondra grins.

'Oh goodness, that will probably scare Cole off forever!' I laugh, but I know she's right.

Cole texts me in the morning to say that tonight will be fine and that he will go to my parents' house directly from the airport. I feel more at ease once I've received his message, and for some reason, I wonder whether he will still feel the same as the day progresses. Then I get annoyed at myself for doubting him. It's in his nature to follow through with whatever commitment he has made. I'm grateful when the phone interrupts my thoughts until I hear the voice on the other end greeting me.

'Good morning, Tali, will you come to the marketing office, please?'

Standing in front of the elevator doors, Number One is the winner today.

Well done, Number One, I say to myself in a Japanese accent.

I laugh out loud as I stare at the doors, wondering what it will be like when the cartoons are up. The elevator stops, and I take a deep breath before walking out and into the marketing office. Josh, Greg, and Brett are examining a large board covered with cartoons. They're all laughing, so I guess Josh approves of their work.

'Hey Tali, this is awesome, I can't believe you came up with this,' Brett says, lifting the board so I can see which one they've finally agreed on.

'Oh, so much for the secrecy, thanks, Josh.' I look at him, and from the look on his face, I can see he knows I'm displeased.

'I'm sorry, Tali, it was a slip of the tongue, but credit must get given where it's due, you know,' he adds sheepishly.

'So, you've decided on this one then?' I say, turning my focus to the board and ignoring Josh's last statement.

I pick up the board, happy to see that they've agreed on my first choice.

'I must admit, it's pretty amusing. Well done, you guys. Think this must be a first in any building ever. Perhaps you should consider patenting the rights to it, Josh? You could become famous one day.' I smile at him, thinking that perhaps I shouldn't always be so sarcastic.

'And if I do, don't think you'll be getting any royalties,' he smirks.

I tell Greg and Brett again that it's a great effort, and then I leave.

'You should see the cartoon for the elevator doors, it's quite brilliant,' I say to Sondra and Cheri as I walk back into the office, 'should be up in about a week.'

'Maybe you'll get a raise as it is your idea!' Cheri says absentmindedly.

RIO ADV
SAFARI RULES

CHAPTER TWELVE

At my parents' house, my mum is, for once, happy that I've brought pizza. She had a busy day full of charity work and was unable to prepare a meal. It feels odd to have takeout in their house, but it's a good change, even for her. Cole will be arriving later, which means his pizza will be cold, but that won't bother him; food is food, as far as he's concerned.

Once he arrives, we settle down in the lounge; Cole and I under a blanket on the sofa, and my mum and dad in their armchairs. Cole has his Bible with him and is very proud to tell us that he looked up all the scriptures my dad gave him on the plane.

Dad prays, and then we begin our study. Again, it amazes me how quickly Cole grasps the concept of the truth. How God sent His only Son to teach the world about His Kingdom, how Jesus died for our sins, was resurrected, and now reigns at God's right hand. Now, we too can have this eternal life through baptism.

While we have a coffee break, my dad asks Cole if he's ready to accept Jesus as his Saviour, to obey the Truth and God's Word.
I hold my breath for a second before he answers.
'I most certainly am. Will you baptize me, Leon?'
My mum and I both yell out with delight, and I throw my arms around Cole, hugging him until he can't breathe.
'I'm so happy, my love,' I whisper into his ear.
'Cole dear, this is wonderful,' my mum is bouncing on her chair with excitement, and I'm sure I detect a tear or two. She gives Cole a hug that seems to last forever.
'I would be delighted to, son, whenever you are ready.'
I can see my dad is jubilant, and if he weren't such a gentleman, he'd be jumping around too.
'Can we do it in the sea, or is that not allowed?'
'Jesus got baptized in a river; the sea will be no different,' my mum answers before any of us can.

'Well, can we go now? I'm afraid to wait until morning; maybe I'll die tonight!'

Cole's eyes are bright as he smiles his huge, beautiful smile; he is clearly so eager, and I cannot help but be in awe of him.

My dad laughs, 'Now is excellent, and the sea awaits us then. We can go to the section of the beach where the floodlights are; they should still be on.'

'Dad, can Cole borrow a pair of shorts and a T-shirt from you? He hasn't got other clothes here.'

'That won't be necessary, love, you know I always have spare clothes in my car. I'm forever getting my clothes wet or full of sand when I go surfing,' he explains to my parents.

We arrive at the beach, and to say it is freezing is most definitely an understatement. However, the clouds have disappeared, and the stars seem to be glowing more brightly than ever.

I have borrowed another jacket from my dad, and now I do look like an Eskimo. I don't envy Cole and my dad, entering into that water, but for one's salvation, freezing is a minor obstacle.

At the water's edge, we stand together, holding hands, while my dad prays for our family, especially for God to accept this new soul into His family. The two men make their way into the water while Mum and I watch, holding towels and jackets ready for Cole's immersion. My mum puts her arm around me, gently and lovingly, and I realize how much this means to her.

'Thanks, Mum; you and Dad are just perfect. I love you.' I tighten my arm around her and bend my head, so it rests on hers.

'This is wonderful. God knows our prayers, and today he's answered mine. I love you too.'

Dad asks Cole if he repents from his sins, and then he asks him if he accepts Jesus as his Saviour.

To both Cole replies, 'Yes,' then Dad submerges him.

Fortunately, it is low tide, so there are barely any waves. A few seconds pass, and Cole comes up, a new man. As he comes towards us from the water, I run towards him and wrap a towel around his shoulders. He is shivering so much his teeth are chattering, and I rub his arms vigorously so he will dry more quickly. Then I bundle him in a jacket and hold him tightly. We have a quick prayer on the beach, then go back to my parents' house.

While I make coffee, Cole showers, and my mum phones Eric. 'Mum, it's late, leave it till the morning,' I say, knowing she won't listen to me.
'No, this is good news, it can't wait,' she speaks into the receiver. 'Hello, Eric dear, guess what? Cole just got baptized in the sea! I know, isn't it wonderful? Well, sleep tight then, love you.' She hangs up and turns back to me.
'Eric is so happy for Cole and says he will give him a call in the morning.'
'Do you think Judith will ever study?' I ask her.
'Well, they haven't been together very long, so let's give it time and see what God has in store. I hope so, though.'
Cole walks into the lounge, fresh and ecstatic. I give him his coffee, put a blanket around him as we sit down on the couch, and kiss him on the cheek.
He turns to look at me, 'I can't tell you how relieved I feel – happy and at peace, but most of all happy.'
He cannot stop smiling. Even as he sips his coffee, it's difficult for him to stop smiling. My dad comes into the lounge after his shower, and Cole puts his mug down, walks over to my dad, and puts his arms around him.
'Thanks, Leon, this is the best thing that's ever happened to me, and I'm very grateful to you and Rose.'
'You have made me very happy tonight, son; God has answered our prayers.'
I cannot stop the tears of joy from sliding down my cheeks.

Eventually, we leave my parents' house to go to mine. As always, I go straight to the kitchen and put the water on to boil. Cole throws his wet clothes in the bath and joins me in the kitchen.
'Now that I'm a Christian...' He puts a lot of emphasis on the word 'Christian,' and smiles, but sounds a little nervous to me. He hesitates, holds my hands in his, and for a few seconds

stares at our joined hands. Then he looks at me, still smiling, still nervous, and says,

'I, um, I want to know, or to ask you, um, if you, or, um, will you marry me? I, um, don't have a ring or anything yet, but, um, I want to check with you, you know, if you want to. I will ask Leon first; then we can maybe make it official, or not, if you want to, um, well, will you, what you think?' He still hasn't taken a breath.

I stare at him, not breathing either.

Did he just propose? In the kitchen? Oh my goodness, yes, he did!

It takes me a few seconds to register what just happened. I scream and throw my arms around him, 'Yes, yes, yes, yes a thousand times yes! Oh, love, I love you and will do it however you want! If you want to ask my dad first, then that's fine, it's the right way, I guess.'

I kiss him, and he kisses me back fervently. At this moment, I know that I love him more than anything and that our life together is going to be perfect.

CHAPTER THIRTEEN

The sun shines into my room through a gap in the blinds and hits me right in the face, waking me up reluctantly. At first, I feel like pulling the duvet over my face and going back to sleep, but Cole is already up and pulls the duvet and blanket off me and drags me by my feet off the bed.

'No, Cole,' I laugh, and screech, 'it's too cold, why do you want to get up now?'

His face is bright and glowing, and he is wearing his beautiful smile. 'Time to get up, we can't sleep all day on the first day of my new life, now can we?'

By now, I'm on the floor trying to curl myself into the blanket that is also on the floor. Cole is quicker than I am, and before I know it, the blanket and I are being dragged to the bathroom. We both laugh like little children in a playground.

'You are so cruel, it's cold, okay, okay, I will get up, I promise!' I say through spouts of laughter.

I stagger in the process of getting up off the floor and look at myself in the bathroom mirror. I cannot believe what horror stares back at me. I am a mess, and no hairstylist, no matter how hard they tried, could ever get my hair to look this crazy.

'Yes, you look a right mess!' Cole stands in the bathroom doorway and grins.

'It's your fault, remember, you will have to look at this face every morning for the rest of your life.' I smile as I think about his proposal the night before.

'Well, I will have the greatest alarm clock because you'll shock me awake for sure!' He bursts out laughing and goes to finish making coffee in the kitchen.

After spending ages in a hot shower, I put on my cuddly bathrobe and Ugg boots. Plodding to the kitchen, I find Cole leaning against the counter, drinking his coffee.

'You feel human? You sure look more human. Coffee?' He points to my cup, and I take it, holding it against my chest with my fingers wrapped around it.

'Thanks. So, what've we got planned for today?' I sense he already has something in mind.

'Well, I thought we could invite our parents to dinner and make it official.'

'Oh, okay,' I reply, not hiding the hesitation in my voice.

'You haven't changed your mind, have you?' He looks worried.

'Oh no, no, not at all, I just didn't think you'd worry about it so soon. You phone your folks, and I'll phone mine.'

I stand in front of him and kiss him on the chin, and then take another sip of coffee.

'The sooner, the better, in my book,' he says, putting his arms around my waist and kissing my forehead, 'shall we make it at six? What are we going to feed them? Mm, maybe you can show me these cooking skills Rose has been bragging about?'

'Can't we just have a barbecue?' I groan.

'It's too cold to stand outside. Oh, we can make pasta, though, nothing fancy, and I'll help you.'

'No, it's okay. I'll make a big special dinner and prove to you that getting married to me is the best investment you will ever make.'

He holds me closer, 'You don't have to prove anything to me.'

We make the calls, and understandably, both sets of parents are curious about the sudden invitation. My parents are easily satisfied with the excuse of celebrating Cole's new life, and he tells his parents that we want to spend time with them before they leave on their next trip, which is in a week, so it is not entirely a lie.

'Should we invite Eric and Garth as well?' I ask, not sure how personal Cole wants this to be.

'Maybe not, think we should make this special, just for our parents. We can visit Garth and Merle tomorrow, and Eric can always meet us there if you like.

'My mom will probably tell Eric before dinner's even made, but it'll be nice to visit Garth and Merle tomorrow. We haven't seen them in a while. Merle can probably not even walk anymore!'

I know Garth and Merle want to tell Cole about naming their child after him, so I guess this will be a good time.

'Hey, buddy, what's up?' I can hear Garth's enthusiastic greeting.

'No great, how's Merle?'

He listens for a while as Garth goes into detail about the latest news about her pregnancy. He's a good listener and a good friend.

'Oh shame, hey, so she's stopped working now, but whatever is best for the baby, hey.'

Cole listens.

'Yeah, you're right. Listen, if you guys are up to it, Tali and I want to come over tomorrow. Whenever suits you.'

Garth is talking again.

'I know I don't have to phone first, but I wasn't sure if you'd have anything else on. Okay, we'll catch you at two then. While the girls gossip, we can grab a wave. Okay, buddy, check you later,' Cole hangs up. 'All the scenarios set then. Should we go shopping?'

'I think we should. If I have to make dinner, we need food, and I also want to get the baby something nice.'

Cole goes surfing while I relax before starting dinner. I'm not exactly looking forward to my mother affirming my cooking skills. I've never made dinner for a special occasion before, so I have to admit to myself that I'm rather nervous. I don't doubt my skills; it's my mother's criticism I fear. Oh yes, I've also never done anything like this for Cole's parents; in fact, neither set of parents has ever been around the same dinner table before. Oh well, if they don't like it, it'll be their problem, not mine, and with this thought, I feel a lot better.

I set my small dining table with the new pale green bamboo placemats and dinnerware we bought earlier today. The plates are white with a thin green bamboo pattern around the edges, which match the placemats perfectly. Cole and I had a wonderful time choosing everything, and fortunately, we discovered that our tastes are very similar.

I make butternut soup to start, and roast chicken braised with honey and mustard for mains, served with roast potatoes, sweet carrots, and peppered green beans. For dessert, I bought a delicious-looking cheesecake.
My father gives thanks, and before anyone has time to start eating, Cole interjects, 'Mom, Dad, I have something to tell you.'
'Pay up, old girl,' Bob says to Jeny and laughs, 'I took a bet with Jeny that something was brewing.'
Jeny smiles. 'Oh, you! Let Cole speak.'
'Last night I was baptized. I've been studying with Leon and, well, I've changed my life now.'
He stops speaking and stares at his parents, not sure of their reactions.
'Well, son, this is good news, I guess, you know, we've never been churchgoers, as a person would say, but if this is the path you want to follow, then I'm happy for you. As I know you, you wouldn't do something that is not right, so good for you, son.'
'That's lovely, son, where did you get baptized?' Jeny sounds genuinely pleased and interested in the details, and Cole gladly explains the entire process during dinner. Bob and Jeny have some questions for my dad, and he, of course, is superb in his replies. While we sit around the table, I suddenly envisage myself as my mother. I've just made a huge meal for the whole family, and they're enjoying it.
She suddenly raises her glass of orange juice and says, 'Here's to Talia-May, who has cooked a wonderful meal, just like I said she could. So, Cole, at least you know you'll never starve.'
They all laugh as I grimace. At least now she has said it. Then Cole stands up, and I feel my cheeks redden, and my stomach fills with butterflies. I have to swallow a giggle that wants to burst out. He really is going to go through with it. He holds his glass in one hand and my hand with the other, nervously playing with my fingers.

'Um, there is another reason you're all here, so pay up, mom,' he smiles at Jeny and turns to my dad, 'Leon, I would like to ask you if I may marry your daughter?'
After a few seconds of silence, the penny drops. My dad stands up and walks around the table to Cole, who looks as though he's about to run a mile. My dad puts his arms around Cole and hugs him, then steps back, holding Cole's shoulders,
'Welcome to the family, my son. Of course, you can.'
'Oh, oh, oh, this is so wonderful!' Of course, my mom is her excitable self as she stumbles up to embrace us.
Bob and Jeny are thrilled.
'You hear that old girl? We might still get grandchildren before we pass on.'
Everyone laughs.
'So, where's the ring?' Jeny asks, 'You're supposed to go on your knees now and propose!'
'I proposed to Tali last night,' Cole blushes, 'but I wanted to ask Leon before telling anyone. And I haven't got a ring yet.'
We spend the rest of the evening talking about weddings. Our parents tell us stories about their respective weddings; it's like being in a time machine, and it's lovely.

CHAPTER FOURTEEN

As excited as I am to be going back to church after so many years, it's still difficult to get out of bed. Especially because it's so cold. Once again, Cole has to drag me out of bed, but at least I am not dragged across the floor this time.

Walking into the church is a strange but comforting feeling. I feel like I've come home; that I've been on a long and arduous journey and have finally arrived. My mum introduces us to almost every single person in the building. There's no conceivable way that I can remember everyone's names; some faces I vaguely recognize, but there are so many new faces, and poor Cole just hovers alongside me.

Finally, we sit down next to my parents, and the service begins. I keep glancing at Cole, trying to make out what he is thinking, but he sits calmly and takes it all in. He is unflustered when Minister Wade welcomes him to God's church and gladly goes forward for a prayer. At tea after the service, he seems to enjoy chattering to the old ladies when they come to congratulate and welcome him. He speaks to the men as though he's been a member of God's family all his life.
Why has it taken us so long to get here? I can't help but muse regretfully.

After a long fellowship with the other members, we make our way to Garth and Merle's. Garth is ready to go surfing and waits for us to arrive impatiently while Merle lies stretched out on the sofa, too large to move.
'About time you guys got here,' Garth mutters reproachfully, 'the swell is great! I was going to go out by myself if you didn't pitch soon!'
'Let's go, just give me a sec to change.'
Cole kisses Merle on the forehead and rushes off to change. It takes Cole no longer than two minutes, and then he kisses me

goodbye and quickly whispers to me that I'm not to say anything until they're back.

I make us tea and squeeze in at Merle's feet on the couch, her body sprawled across most of it. We chat mainly about her pregnancy and how excited she is to meet her little boy. I cannot believe how big her belly has grown since I last saw her. According to the doctors, she still has three weeks left, but she wouldn't mind if the baby came today.

The men have not gone long when they return with long faces. The swell wasn't as great as Garth had thought. Soon, we are relaxing in the lounge with glasses of wine, warm in front of the fireplace.
'So, Cole, we've got something to tell you.' Garth stands up and goes to sit on the floor in front of Merle, 'We are going to name the baby Cole, after you. That cool with you?'
Cole stares at them both, dumbfounded.
'You're kidding me, seriously? That is awesome! Ah man, this kid is going to be a legend!' He laughs and gets up to hug them, 'Thanks, buddy, I feel genuinely touched, man.'
It's so good to see the honest affection he and Garth share.
'Okay, so now it's my turn for an announcement.'
He hesitates, seemingly a little unsure of how his best friend will react.
'On Friday night, I got baptized. Tali's dad has been studying with me, and we went to the beach and did it in the sea. This morning I went to church with Tali.'
There is a brief silence while it's their turn to absorb the news.
'Wow? Hey, that's good man, I know you'd never do anything you don't believe in, so I'm happy for you.'
'That's wonderful, Cole, congrats, hey!' Merle says without moving from her position on the couch.
'Okay, so that's not all, I've got more news,' Cole pauses to prolong the anticipation. Then smiling, he comes over to me, sits on the arm of my chair, and picks up my hand, 'We got engaged too. Well, I asked Tali to marry me, and last night I asked Leon, and he gave us his blessing, so now I have to get a ring!' He stops and lets out a long breath.

'Oh my word, oh my word! Tali! And you sat here the whole time and never said a word. This is such fantastic news, you guys!' Merle heaves herself off the sofa.

'Awesome man, I knew it would happen soon enough. Well done, buddy!' Garth grins delightedly.

It's a wonderful thing to have such close friends. We laugh a lot during the rest of the visit – about Merle's inability to move, what the baby will look like, and how he's going to grow up to become a superstar, super surfer, and all-around good guy because he's named Cole.

CHAPTER FIFTEEN

It's still dark outside; winter isn't officially here yet, so why is it so cold? Hurriedly, I make my way to the bathroom and yell at Cole, who's already banging around in the kitchen, to hurry up with the coffee. He yells something back, but I can't make out, having already shut the bathroom door. Once I've finished showering and go back into the bedroom, I find a mug of steaming coffee standing on my bedside table.
I chuckle to myself and think, *Boy, have I got him well trained already.*

I put on tights under my jeans, a thick brown polo-neck jersey, a chunky parka jacket, and boots. I know I look completely ridiculous, but that is not the problem; it's keeping warm that is.

Walking up to the entrance of the office building, I see Booker standing outside as usual.
Booker's blood must be so thick, I think to myself.
He opens the door for me, laughing like he did the other day, and just like that day, I'm not very amused.
'Booker, how was your weekend?' He walks in behind me, and I feel the need to tell him about my weekend.
'It was good as always, Miss Medeck. I try to relax as much as possible on weekends, and it's not always easy with a house full of young ones.'
'I can imagine. Are you a Christian by the way, do you go to church?' I blurt out curiously.
'Oh yes, I most definitely am, and I most definitely do, never miss it for anything.'
'Well, a very good thing happened to me this weekend, Cole got baptized on Friday night.'
'God works in the most wonderful ways, not for us to understand or to question.'

'Very true, you're the first person I've told here, so you should feel honored,' I joke, and Booker braggingly poses as I head for the elevator.

While I wait for elevator Number One to arrive, I think about how easy it is to talk to Booker. Number One arrives, *Well done, Number One,* (Jamaican accent.)

As usual, when I get into the office, I put my things on my desk and head straight to the coffee machine. I open the blinds and stare out at the grey day outside. It looks as though it's going to start raining any minute, though it feels more like snow is on its way. Sondra and Cheri interrupt my thoughts as they walk in, praising Booker for warming up the office so comfortably.

'So, hello ladies, I bet neither of you had a weekend as good as I did?' I'm bubbling with excitement.

'He proposed?' Sondra's response is the same as always, so she doesn't expect me to reply positively. When I do, it takes her by complete surprise.

'Yes, he did! Can you believe it? He did!' I'm almost shouting. They both grab my hands and look for a ring.

'He hasn't got the ring yet, but he did pop the question, almost right after he got baptized.' I emphasize the word 'baptized,' so they can hear it clearly over their excitement.

'He what?' They say in unison.

'Yeah, on Friday night! While we were studying, he decided he didn't want to wait any longer. So, we went to the beach, and my dad baptized him in the sea. It was so cold but so very special, and then when we eventually got home, he asked me to marry him. We haven't set a date yet or anything, and on Saturday night, we had the parents over for dinner, and Cole told them. They were all thrilled, especially my mother, of course.'

'Wow, we're so happy for you, Tali! We need to celebrate! Let's go to Shakes for lunch.' Cheri looks at Sondra, who eagerly nods.

When they get to their desks, both message Cole to congratulate him on both occasions. While I'm working on the Select Foods account again, which always seems to be a problem, a Skype message pops up on my screen. It's from Josh, and immediately I feel uneasy; what idiotic thing have I gone and done now?

Congratulations on your engagement. I'm sure you and Cole will be very happy together.

'What have you two done?' I ask loudly, 'Who all have you told, and how?'

Cheri and Sondra laugh loudly and exclaim together, 'Everyone!'

'Well, thanks for that, just got a message from Josh.'

'Oh, well, we didn't tell him actually,' Sondra is surprised, 'but then again, nothing stays a secret for long in this place.'

I Skype him back:

Thank you very much. There is no ring yet, but I'm sure you will get that news as soon as it happens.

CHAPTER SIXTEEN

One Sunday afternoon, Cole and I are relaxing at his flat when he suddenly jumps up off the couch and suggests we go to the beach. It's not exactly a sunny day, but the surf is supposed to be good, and Cole is adamant that I go with him. It is not like him, but I don't take much notice. Instead, I grab my thick parka jacket, put on a beanie, gloves, and a scarf, and slip on my Ugg boots.
'Dressed for the North Pole again?' Cole grins as we leave.

While Cole is in the water, I daydream and stare at the sea, thinking that even with a wetsuit on, Cole must be freezing in the water. I convince myself there and then that all surfers must be immune to the cold. It is just humanly impossible not to freeze in this cold weather and the even colder water.

Cole comes running out of the water, surfboard under his arm. The waves have disappeared, which means it's over for the day. He rolls down the top of his wetsuit, hurriedly dries himself with a towel, and puts on a sweater. I get up, presuming we will leave immediately, but he's busy looking for something in his bag. Eventually, he seems to find what he's looking for and jumps up, smiling at me.
'What's it?' I'm confused.
'Hope you like it,' he says, handing me a little box, 'I know you've already said yes, but will you marry me?'
'I, um, you, you bought a ring? Cole!' I exclaim, opening the box.
It is too beautiful—the ring sparkles in the light. Set in white gold, there's a diamond, at least, half a carat, in the shape of a teardrop.
'It is, wow, um, Cole, when did you?' I cannot get a decent sentence out. What a magnificent ring. All I can do is kiss him and hug him. He slips the ring on my finger, and it fits perfectly.

'I saw it in a shop and knew you liked the shape because you liked those earrings so much that I gave you.'
'Cole, you are full of surprises lately! It must've cost you a fortune!'
'That's not a worry; you're worth it.'

Back at his flat, I cannot stop myself from looking at the ring from all angles. I hold my hand up in front of me and admire the way the diamond sparkles.
I laugh out loud, 'Wait until Cheri and Sondra see it tomorrow!'
'Don't say anything; see how long it takes for them to notice.'
'I can promise you it'll take Sondra seconds; she doesn't miss a thing like this! You'd better get prepared for Thursday night; my mum is going to go crazy again.'
We make our way to the couch with dinner and wine and snuggle in front of the TV, happy.

It's July now, and time seems to be passing more and more quickly by the day. Cole and I are growing in our faith on a daily basis. We read our Bibles and pray every morning before we do anything else. At first, I thought Cole might be embarrassed to pray together, but what was I thinking? This is Cole! He took to it as though he'd done it all his life. We've joined a young adults' group at the church and are enjoying our newfound friends and the studies that are perfectly suited to our needs. It's essential to fellowship with Christians our age, although Garth and Merle are and will always be our best friends.
One particular evening, while we're playing pool in the game room at church, Cole's cell phone rings. He excuses himself to answer it. From across the room, I see his face go pale and then brighten.
He hangs up, 'Merle's in labor, Tali! Garth asked if we could meet him at the hospital, he's freaking out a little!'
'Of course! Oh goodness, let's hurry,' I say excitedly.
Our friends ask us to convey their best wishes to Garth and Merle and congregate together on the couches to pray for Garth, Merle, and the baby. We race to the hospital, thankfully

only about five kilometers away, and run into the maternity ward. We're not sure whether we'll be permitted into the ward because we're not immediate family, but Garth has left a notice at the staff desk to allow us in. We wait in the waiting room, and a nurse goes in to call Garth. It's not long before he comes rushing out of the ward, looking pale and panicky.

'So glad you guys are here. With neither of our parents around, I sure need you guys.'

'How's Merle doing?' I ask, interrupting him.

'She's been going now for four hours; the doctor says it should be any time now.'

'That's rather quick, isn't it? I've heard of women going on for eleven hours,' I watch Garth worriedly as he paces back and forth, obviously wanting to get back to Merle.

'Yeah, they say she's a natural. Listen, I'm going back to her, but you guys just wait here, please. I'll come out when I can. Hope you don't mind, it's good to know you're here.'

'Hey, you get back to Merle, we'll be right here. Just let us know as soon as Cole Jnr arrives.'

As Garth rushes back to Merle, I notice Cole's excitement growing as we wait. Thankfully, there's a coffee machine in the waiting room, and we immediately make ourselves a cup. We hold hands and say a prayer for our friends and a healthy baby, then settle into the worn armchairs and wait anxiously. After about an hour, Garth comes rushing through the door again.

There are tears in his eyes.

Is something wrong? I'm too afraid to ask.

He stands in the doorway, his head bent, and then he looks up, and I see tears streaming down his face. I'm sure something is wrong.

What can I say to him? How do I react to such news?

'Cole Jnr is here; he's so tiny and so perfect. I'm a father!' He cries out amid his tears and comes towards us, arms open.

Cole gets up and hugs Garth like a brother, 'Well done, buddy, congrats!'

'How is Merle?' I ask, hugging Garth too, 'Congratulations, I'm so happy for you.'

'She's doing well, glad it's all over. She will be in the ward in about half an hour, and then you can see her.'

'Are you sure, don't you want the time to yourselves?' I feel as though Cole and I may be intruding on their exceptionally intimate moment.

'No, really, Merle has asked for you already.'

Garth leaves again. We wait for another hour before he comes out to fetch us. Walking very quietly into the ward, I'm afraid we'll make too much noise and disturb Merle or Cole Jnr. As we approach her, Garth goes straight to Merle's side, takes her hand, and kisses her. I feel like an intruder in this very tender, touching, and deeply personal moment of their lives.

Merle looks up at us and smiles.

'Thanks for coming. Garth needed some moral support. I was not exactly pleasant back there. Come and meet your godchild.'

Merle holds him out for Cole to take him. Cole looks unsure at first, but once he has the tiny bundle in his arms, nothing else seems to matter, and he stares at the child with tears glistening in his eyes. I have to wait for ages before I get a chance to hold him.

As I look at him, I think, *How perfect he is, he's got all ten fingers and all ten toes.* We are born so perfect in God's image, and an overwhelming feeling envelopes me as I stare at this miracle lying so contentedly in my arms.

Sadly, we are not allowed to stay very long. Merle gets tired quickly, and the nursing staff grow agitated because we are holding them up. Before we leave, Cole asks if he may say a prayer for Cole Jnr. We all hold hands, bow our heads, and Cole brings this tiny gift before God, asking Him to bless him and his parents. Cole asks that God give Garth and Merle knowledge and guidance and that He will show them the way to salvation, that they might raise Cole Jnr in a manner pleasing to Him.

Cole and I stroll to his car, thanking the nursing staff for their kindness on the way out. As we walk, we cannot stop talking about Cole Jnr. We discuss his tiny feet, his perfectly formed hands, whose eyes he has, that he has Garth's chin, how well Merle looks so soon after giving birth, and how Garth thinks he deserves all the credit.

Thursday night at my parents' provides new and interesting conversations. Mum, Judith, and I chat about Cole Jnr and how Sondra and Cheri took three days to notice my ring. We seem to bore the men who change the subject at every opportunity. We also discuss my team-building event with the company, which is taking place on the weekend. Cole is terribly jealous and keeps offering advice on how to abseil properly and how to make sure I know what equipment they should be using. My dad is excited about the upcoming men's lectureship in the first week of August in Bloemfontein; he asks Cole to join him, and Cole is delighted. I smile as Cole asks all sorts of questions about what to expect and what happens at these kinds of events. My dad, having been to every single one since the inception, enjoys reminiscing about past lectureships and fills Cole's mind with all sorts of interesting pieces of information.

CHAPTER SEVENTEEN

I am greeted at the office on Friday morning by a mass of chaos. The Overlander truck, which we will be traveling to Table Mountain on tomorrow morning, is parked in front of the building, and it seems like hundreds of people are milling around it.

I park my car and dash to the foyer so as not to be in the cold air for too long. As always, Booker is waiting to greet me. We chat briefly about the hike and the abseiling; he has never done abseiling before, but the hike will be a piece of cake for him. Elevator Number Two is the chosen one (in a Swedish accent), although Number One is the winner. I step into the elevator and turn around to face the doors.
'Oh my goodness!' I gasp. The cartoon is on the door, and it looks awesome. It's brilliant, and finally, I have to admit to myself that I am a genius, so I proudly rub my imaginary Noddy badge in approval.

Not much work gets done today. I keep being interrupted by everyone who's been in the elevator, praising me for the cartoons. Everyone seems to be in good spirits with tomorrow's trip looming. Shelly, one of the tour guides, has taken a bet with Booker on who will reach the top first. Most of us have bet on Booker, but this makes Shelly even more determined to beat him.
Just before we leave work, Josh sends a Skype message to everyone:
I'm looking forward to tomorrow, and would like to thank everyone for your enthusiasm, PS!! How about the excellent elevator doors? See you all tomorrow.

I want to have an early night, but Cole's parents are leaving this evening, and Hungary is their chosen destination this time. Their flight is at 20:00, which means we have to be at the airport by 18:00. I have just enough time to get to Cole's flat before we leave for Bob and Jeny's. They are like children excited about going to a party. They keep going over their lists of places to visit and places to stay. Finally, they've boarded, and we're on our way back to Cole's.

'When we retire, I want to be like your parents; I want to travel and see all these interesting places they have always talked about; it always sounds like they have so much fun!'

Cole nods his head in agreement. I look at my cellphone; it's flat again.

'Please remind me to put my cell phone on charge when we get home, I've let it go flat again.'

'One day you are going to miss a very important call,' he reprimands me.

When we get home, I duly put my cell phone on charge and lie down on the couch. It's not long, and I'm asleep, Cole next to me.

It is awful to wake up at 04:30. If Cole weren't with me, I would snuggle under my duvet and carry on sleeping. He kindly reminds me why I am getting up so early and drags me out of bed with the promise of a cup of fresh coffee. He drives me to Rio Adventures, and I feel bad that he is not joining us, but the feeling does not last long. As he parks outside the gate and I see the big Overlander ready and waiting for us, I bounce around excitedly, say goodbye to Cole in the car, and walk into the yard.

Shelly is trying to up the stakes on her and Booker's bet with anyone who will listen. June is standing next to Booker, a little nervous, but as colorful as always. We've all received backpacks with the company logo on. Each bag contains energy drinks, biscuits, a cap with the company logo, a map, and a small greeting card with an encouraging message from the De Lucases. Josh arrives, casually dressed, yet still immaculate.

How does he get that right? I wonder.

'Hello, Tali, are you ready to start walking for a few hours? I believe the weather is going to be kind to us, thank goodness.'

'Hi, Josh, kind or not, it's still freezing. I cannot imagine how cold it is going to be up on the mountain.'
'You will be so hot from all the walking; you won't even notice the cold.'
'You don't know me very well! Guess we'd better get going,' I say and head for the Overlander, not wanting to get too involved in a conversation out in the cold, or with Josh for that matter.
'Yes, I think you're right,' he mumbles and asks everyone to get in so we can leave.

The drive to Table Mountain goes by so quickly that by the time we arrive, everyone is still excitedly debating whether Booker or Shelly is going to win. We tumble out of the van and, at the base of the mountain, head up the hiking path in single file. Booker grins at Josh and increases his pace. Shelly, watching Booker very closely, follows on his tail. We giggle at them and keep to our steady pace. Booker is tipping Shelly by two to one, and my bet is, of course, on Booker. Before long, the two of them are out of sight. June sticks with Cheri, Sondra, and me as the climb gets more intense; she seems to be progressively battling to cope. We don't mind her slow pace and lag behind with her, not in any rush to get to the top.

What beauty surrounds us as we climb, climb, and climb some more. As I leave Cheri and Sondra with June and walk ahead, I think to myself that there is just no way a person can deny that God created all this.
Catching up to Josh, he interrupts my thoughts as though he were reading them, 'It's magnificent, isn't it? How do you compare this to the view we had in Hermanus?'
'You can't,' I reply. 'They're both equally stunning. I can never get enough of such beauty.'
'Thanks for hanging back with June; she's a real trooper even if she's slow.'
'That's what it's all about, though, isn't it? Team effort!'
'Yes, exactly. Who's your bet on?' Josh grins conspiratorially.

'Booker. He runs like the wind, and I've no doubt he can hike the same way. I can't wait for the abseiling part.' I pant as we head up a steep bit of the mountain.
'It's an incredible experience.'

Greg and Brett wait for all of us slackers to catch up with them, and for the remainder of the hike, we walk along as a team and share some life stories. Clyde is far more relaxed than we've ever known him to be, and he, too, shares some of his adventures. At one stage, as Clyde describes an incident in Botswana, we have to stop walking; we are laughing so hard. At times, we stop to let June catch her breath as we admire a special plant or animal Clyde points out. He gives us engaging lessons on the fauna and flora we encounter, as well as a history lesson about the first cable cars and how they got built. Listening to him helps the time go by more quickly, and even June forgets she is struggling to walk up the never-ending incline of Table Mountain.

After three hours, we eventually arrive at the top of the mountain. All of us are hot and sweaty, so, as Josh predicted, the cold is no longer a concern. Booker and Shelly are already waiting for us to join them. Shelly is inspecting a flowering bush while Booker is having a nap on a patch of grass.

Most of us collapse on the ground, realizing our muscles have done more these past few hours than they have done in years. Some remain standing, too tired to do anything else.
'So, who won?' Brett asks.
'I did!' Shelly exclaims triumphantly.
'She is such a liar!' A voice comes from the body on the lawn. Booker stands up and raises both arms into the air.
'I beat Shelly by at least five minutes!'
We all look to Shelly, who laughs and shrugs her shoulders, 'Yeah, he is right, sorry if you lost your money.'
Forgetting their aching muscles, everyone rushes around confirming who lost and who won what. We laugh with excitement as we give Booker high fives and congratulate the proud man with a huge grin spread across his face.

On top of the mountain, there is a museum and a restaurant that has prepared lunch for us all. We get treated to a delicious vegetable soup with freshly baked bread and a beef stew. The aroma greets us as we enter the restaurant, and I realize how hungry I am. Booker is asked to bless the food, and while we eat, we chatter about the eagerly anticipated abseiling.

After lunch, we stroll through the museum for a bit; it truly is fascinating. June, Clyde, and Shelly share historical facts with us, and we are in awe of the history and beauty that this most magnificent creation holds.

At last, we make our way to the cable car area, where the abseiling will take place.

The question on everyone's lips is, 'Who is going first?'

Josh insists on going last so he can be sure everyone gets down safely. Clyde agrees to go first so that he'll be at the base waiting for us. Then the debating becomes annoying as to who will go next, so I volunteer to get away from the bickering. Unsurprisingly, no one argues.

Gingerly, I walk to the edge of the mountain, not quite ready to look down. The instructor fits me with a harness and, as he briefed Clyde, explains what to do and what to expect. Finally, it is time. I slowly move closer to the edge and, as I look down, am overwhelmed by a feeling of vertigo. Suddenly, I panic and take a few hurried steps back. Immediately, Josh is at my side.

'Are you okay? Are you sure you want to go now? It will be okay. Just remember to do what they told you.' He grabs my arm and reassures me.

'Thanks, Josh,' I laugh it off, feeling embarrassed. 'I will be fine; I was not expecting that urge to fall forward to be so strong. Maybe you should warn the others that it will happen. I'm okay now, though; I'm ready.'

'Enjoy it, Tali; you're a real trooper.'

He touches my arm again and then returns to the others. They watch me move to the jump-off point again, and I stand dead still and say a quick prayer to myself. Everyone yells out words of encouragement as they watch me, wondering if they will be able to go through with it. The cars below look like dinky little

cars; it is incredibly high, but the adrenaline starts taking over, and now I am more than ready to go. It is now or never. Turning around, I slowly step off the edge of the mountain. One step at a time, and I begin my descent. Soon, it becomes so exhilarating that I get more and more confidence. I push my feet up against the edge of the mountain and kick off again, sliding down the rope. I feel like a professional! It's so incredible, and whenever I dare sneak a peek over my shoulder, the scenery is breathtaking. I feel the wind – quite strong in certain places – lash out at my cheeks, and I don't mind one bit. All too soon, I reach the bottom and, looking up, I see some of the others already on their way down. June went after me and is already halfway down. One by one, my colleagues join me, with the same reaction every time – complete and utter exhilaration, what a total rush. The consensus is that we would do it again in a heartbeat. Eventually, Josh reaches the bottom too and is as excited as the rest of us, though he has done it before.
'It's always amazing; no matter how many times you do it!' He states his opinion, which is probably true, and I nod.

Very reluctantly, we make our way to the Overlander, again talking nonstop about our adventure. We all agree that skydiving should be next on our 'to-do' list. Josh promises to discuss it with his father. Surprisingly, the trip home is quiet. I am sure everyone is wrapped up in their thoughts, and probably, like me, replaying the whole day over and over in their minds.

Driving into the yard, I see Cole waiting for me. When I get out of the Overlander, I go straight over to him, kiss him, and tell him how wonderful it was. He laughs and says he can well believe me.
Josh comes over to us, shakes Cole's hand, and greets him warmly.
'Tali here is our star; she showed everyone how it gets done!'
'Oh, Josh, don't exaggerate, but it was so much fun!' I turn to Cole, my eyes shining.

'Well, I no doubt will hear all about it tonight, tomorrow night, and about every other night for weeks to come,' Cole says jokingly and pulls me to him tightly, an arm around my waist.

'Thanks for today, Josh, it was out of this world, and please thank Mr. De Luca for me too.'

'Thanks, Tali, it was a really good day indeed. I will be sure to let my dad know it was a great success.'

I say goodbye to everyone and leave with Cole, and, just as he said, I speak about it that night, the next night, the night after that, and a few nights after that. My enthusiasm is kindly tolerated.

CHAPTER EIGHTEEN

Cole's excitement about his trip with my dad to the men's lectureship increases daily; this sparks my dad's enthusiasm, and so my mum and I have to cope with two very happy men in our homes. Cole is almost always happy at any rate, but I think if it were possible, he might just explode! Dad usually flies every year, but since Cole is going along, he wants to make a road trip out of it. My mum and I tease them about their bonding, but our efforts have little effect on them, and they embrace the idea gladly.

The evening of their departure, my mum makes them each a flask of coffee and packs a basket filled to the brim with biscuits, chips, fruit, and sugar sweets – to keep them awake while driving. She fusses over my dad's clothes as she packs for him, adding extra bedding for both of them. It does not help to try to heed her, as it just makes her even more determined not to forget anything.

Eric and Judith arrive, and while Judith and I make a light dinner, the men sit in the lounge and chat on the subject of the route Dad and Cole are going to take. Cole has absolutely no sense of direction and listens to my dad and Eric map the route. I dared to ask why they were bothering, as they have the GPS rigged up in the car. All I got was the evil eye, so I thought it best to leave them to their games since it seems to make them happy.

After hamburgers and salad, we all relax for an hour or so in the lounge before my dad says it's time for them to be on their way. It feels odd to say goodbye to Cole. In the three years we've been together, we've never been apart for such a long period before, even if it's only a week! A strange sensation flows through me, a feeling of both sadness and joy. I'm sad because I will miss Cole, but happy because he's so excited about the prospect of what he is going to experience. After fond farewells, they drive away. Cole is at the wheel, having offered to take the first shift while he is still familiar with the roads. He teased, saying he could not promise where they would land up once he got into unfamiliar territory. He will leave that section of the trip to my dad. I thought that was why they have the GPS!

I stay at my mum's for the night, as it's rather late and I don't feel like being alone. We climb into her bed with Horlicks and chat for hours about our men, reminisce over my and Eric's childhood, my parents' days of courting, and my mum's childhood. As we doze off, I realize what a very special moment this is. It has been many, many years since my mum and I shared such quality time together. I feel like a teenager again, waiting until my dad gets home from some or other church event while lying in bed with my mum.
'This is great, Mum; we haven't done this in ages. I never realized how much I missed it,' I snuggle under the duvet next to her and put my arm around her.
She pats my hand, 'Yes, it has been ages, such a pity you kids have to grow up. Sleep tight; I love you.'
'Love you too, Mum.'
My cell phone blares just as I am about to fall asleep in a perfectly comfortable position.
'Can you believe it?' I mumble as I turn over to reach for it on the nightstand. There's no reply from my mum, who is already fast asleep.
Shame, she must be so tired, I think to myself.
Naturally, the message is from Cole:
Going well, Leon snores so loud lol! Missing u already, luv u sleep tight.
I cannot help giggling, and I know that I would rather be disturbed at any time of the day or night than not hear from him.
Just about to doze off, plse drive safe, in bed with my mum, luv u so much, chat 2moro. I message him back.
I put the phone back on the nightstand, cuddle under the duvet, and am asleep within minutes.

The church is empty on Sunday as most of the men and their families have gone to the lectureship. All the same, it is worth every minute to get fed God's Word and be amongst such wonderful people. I don't stay long afterward, as I want to get home, relax, and sleep the rest of the day away. After speaking to Cole for over an hour, this is what I do. He is on such a spiritual high. He describes almost every minute since their arrival, from the family they are staying with to the food and the studies they will be doing. Mostly, he talks about the singing and the worship they've done. He tells me how thrilled he is to have bumped into the two men who were instrumental in his salvation – Nick Drummond and Henry Lategan. They were equally happy to see him. After introducing them to my dad, the four of them are getting on well and have spent most of their time together. I can hear in his voice that he is a different man, filled with God's Holy Spirit. I miss him so much, though.

It feels like the week without Cole and my dad will never end. I always feel as though I've forgotten something or that I should be doing something else. Even dinner with my mum on Thursday night is quiet and somber. My mum is still as happy and bubbly as ever, but you can feel the absence of Cole and my dad like a thick fog that won't evaporate. Finally, it is time for them to come home. They are going to stay over in Colesberg as they did on the trip up, so it won't be too long before they are home again. I cannot wait.

CHAPTER NINETEEN

When I wake up, the first thing I do is check my cell phone for any messages from Cole. The battery is flat again.

Why do I always do this?

Quickly, I jump out of bed and put it on charge. After a shower and a cup of coffee, I'm sure I'll be able to switch it on to get my messages. Today is Monday and a public holiday; I am so relaxed and happy that Cole will finally be coming home. Eventually, I'm dressed and enjoying a cup of steaming coffee. I switch my cell phone on, and there are only two voice messages from my mum:

Talia-May, please come to my house as soon as you get this.

The second message is almost identical. She doesn't sound any different from how she usually does, so I presume my dad and Cole are almost home, and she wants me to come over.

As I arrive at my parents' house, I notice that Eric and Minister Wade's cars are parked outside.

This will be a nice welcome home for them, I think, as I park behind Eric's car, so he will not be able to move his.

Eric is standing at the sliding door with his head bowed, and I'm surprised to see Judith rubbing his back. Minister Wade is standing in the kitchen, awfully close to my mum.

'Hello, Mum! Hey Eric, Judith. Hello Minister Wade.' I greet everyone in one breath as I put my bag down on the table near the front door and bend down to greet Jack. Eric doesn't answer, and Judith mutters something incoherent.

'Talia-May,' my mum says, 'we have some news.'

Immediately, I think maybe Eric and Judith just got engaged, but before I can say anything, Minister Wade asks me to sit down.

'I'm fine, what's going on?' I ask, suddenly aware that things do not look or feel normal.

As Minister Wade begins to speak, I feel my heart racing. I hear my heart beating in my chest and blood pounding in my ears. His mouth is moving, but I can no longer hear what he is saying. It feels like there's not enough air in the room, and doubling over, I clutch my stomach. Although I can't hear a word of what Minister Wade is saying anymore, I can see Eric crying and Judith gently trying to console him.

'No, no, NO, NO, NO, NO,' I scream, wishing the hammering in my head would stop.

I sink to the floor as everything around me starts to spin.

'NO, NO, NO,' is all I can emit in gasping, raspy whispers.

Minister Wade bends down and tries to put his arms around me, but I shove him away.

'NO, NO, NO,' I yell, again and again until I cannot breathe and my voice is hoarse.

'Talia-May, my darling, it will be all right. Your dad and Cole are with God now, where they belong.'

'WHAT? How? How, how can you say that?' I sob, and the tears stream down my cheeks, 'I don't want them to be with God! I want them to be with me! WITH ME! WITH ME!'

Spit flies off my tongue, and I am barely aware of the hysteria building up inside me. I have no means of controlling it, so I just let it take over. Eric slides to the floor too, his sobbing getting louder and louder in my head. I vaguely see Judith crouch next to him and whisper meaningless words meant to comfort him. Amidst his tears, Eric looks at me wordlessly. His face crumples, and I watch him battle not to become hysterical himself.

'There's a mistake,' I manage to utter. 'There has got to be a mistake. It can't be true; I won't believe it, I WON'T, I WON'T.'

'Talia-May, my love, it's true, I wish it weren't, but it is.'

'Then why are you so calm? WHY ARE YOU NOT UPSET?' I yell, the anger seeping in between the hysteria.

My mother is poised, her chin tilted up, and her eyes are shining.

'I will cry when the time is my own, Talia-May. But I know that they are with God, which is why we live, dear. I can't be sad when I know they are with our Father in Heaven. We should be rejoicing, dear.'

'THEN YOU REJOICE BY YOURSELF!' I yell at her hysterically and sob uncontrollably.

My tears flow like a river burst into a flood, and there is no stopping them.

'NO, NO, NO, NO,' is all I scream out between the wracking sobs.

Minister Wade again tries to console me, and I hear him assure me that everything will be all right. His words are in vain, and I tell him so. I will not listen. I cannot listen!

Eric pulls himself up from the floor and comes over to me. He whispers, 'Tali,' and hugs me, sobbing as hard as I am. We hold each other for what seems like hours, not saying a word but just crying in each other's arms.

I vaguely hear a knock at the door and see my mum let Dr. Ashton in. He speaks to us calmly, but we continue to sob, not hearing a word he says. Through my tears, I see him hand my mum some pills, and I hear him suggest we take them immediately. Eric reluctantly lets go of me and, covering his face, goes to the bathroom. In my daze, my mum hands me the pills, and I swallow them.

'I will have to phone Bob and Jeny. How do I tell them this?' My heart aches, and I splutter as I mouth the words while I get up and go to lie on the couch. I put the pillow over my head, trying to block everything out. I do not want to believe this is happening. Maybe I will wake up from this nightmare, and everything will be back to normal. My mum's voice brings me back to reality.

'You can phone them later, Talia-May. I will be with you when you phone if you want,' my mum sinks into the couch next to me and gently strokes my arm.

All I can do is cry. My heart feels like a heavy stone lying at my feet, and my body shakes as sobs heave from deep within my soul.

Slowly, as I feel the pills taking effect, I find my body relaxing and my mind growing calmer. I lie dead still on the couch and allow the medicine to rush through my blood and do its job. I am exhausted and drained of all energy. I feel hopeless and alone. My mum is on the phone every five minutes, as people receive the news and phone to offer their sympathies. Finally, I

muster up the courage to ask, although I don't want to know the truth. I still hope that I will find out everyone is lying to me and that Cole is not dead. When I think of my dad gone too, I choke but manage to utter the words, 'Tell me what happened.'
Minister Wade sits down on the floor next to the couch and takes my hand in his. Eric and Judith remain at the sliding door, trying to avoid having to hear the story again.
'They left Colesberg early this morning, at about 05:00. Fifteen kilometers outside of Colesberg, a taxi lost control around a corner and hit them head-on. There were no survivors in the taxi either. Leon and Cole died instantly, so they suffered no pain. I'm so sorry, Tali. I know it's hard to understand or make sense of, but we've got to hold on to the fact that they are with God now. There is no pain for them, only joy and laughter. Try to hold onto this truth.'
I see his eyes glisten as he turns to look at Eric, too. 'Tali, I'm always here for you and Eric, if you ever need me.'

I am so grateful when he stops talking. I can't hear anymore. The images flooding through my mind are too much to bear. My beautiful Cole, lying lifeless in a mangled car, my father, my gentle father, lying next to him. It is just not fair.
'Why, why would God take them now? Cole's new life had just begun! Why would He let that happen?'
I look beseechingly at Minister Wade, pleading with him to give me an answer that will allow me to make sense of it all. I ask even though I know there is no answer, only acceptance – which I am not sure I am capable of right now.
'Tali, you know we don't have the answers to things that happen beyond our control. We can only accept that God is in control and rejoice that Leon and Cole are with Him right now.'
I bury my face in my hands and shake my head.
The only words I can muster are, 'It's not fair, it's just not fair.'
'I know my dear, I know,' Minister Wade looks tenderly at me, all out of comforting words to say.
How do I tell Garth? I suddenly think to myself. *Oh no, poor Garth is going to be devastated. How will he take such news?*

*And Merle? Such a shock might upset her feeding Cole Jnr.
Cole Jnr, he will never get to know his godfather.*
These thoughts haunt me as I drift in and out of reality. I try to
make up the sentences to tell them the news – something that
will have the least impact and sound the least shocking.
*Maybe if I tell them soon, it will be better to get it over with?
How can I tell them anything, when every time I open my
mouth, I cry?*

I drag myself up from the couch and go over to Eric and Judith
and put my arms around them. Judith has been so good to Eric,
holding him and comforting him; we remain standing in our
embrace, unseeingly staring outside. My mum joins us and
tries to reassure us, over and over, that everything will be okay.
I cannot understand how positive she is, how unaffected she
seems to be by the loss of her husband of forty-one years. She
keeps telling me that she is rejoicing; that he is where he has
wanted to be all his life. She says she will mourn when she is
ready. I think her reaction to this tragedy is just not normal.

I know I should phone Bob and Jeny while everyone is with
me, so, holding my breath, I dial Bob's number. Since they
have the roaming service on their cell phone, I dial his local
number, but it goes straight to voicemail.
*Oh no, I really want to have this phone call now and not
postpone it.*
I cannot prolong this agonizing over their reaction much
longer. I leave a message for them to phone me back as soon as
possible. I know they will suspect something because, for one,
I never call them; it's always Cole, and secondly, we never call
them while they are on holiday. I hang up and pray it won't be
long before they call back.

Garth. He will need to hear this face-to-face. I know it and
excuse myself. My mother tries to argue that I am in no state to
drive, and Minister Wade kindly suggests that he come with
me. I decline his offer and say I'll phone him if necessary. I get
into my car and start it. My legs start shaking so much that I

can only switch it off and go back inside, realizing that my mother is right, and I am in no state to drive.

I sit back on the couch and bury my head in a cushion. I hope that if I close my eyes and don't move a muscle, this will all go away.
Suddenly, my phone rings. It is Bob. My heart starts racing, and my breathing becomes erratic. Eric, realizing who the caller is, comes to me and takes my free hand.
He suggests, 'You don't have to answer. Phone them back later,'
Shaking my head, I stare at the flashing screen, 'The sooner I get this call over with, the better.'
I take a deep breath, clear my throat, and answer, 'Hello Bob.'
'Hello Tali, we got your message. What's wrong?' I can hear he knows something is wrong by the tone of his voice.
I manage to say his name before bursting into tears again.
Eric gently pries the phone from my fingers and hands it to Minister Wade to handle the rest of the conversation. Minister Wade heads outside to break the news to Bob.
After several minutes, he comes back with my cell phone and says they will phone me later or tomorrow and let me know the soonest they can come home.
'Will they be all right? Cole is their only child,' I ask, wishing I could've been strong enough to give them the news myself.
'Bob did not take it too well, Tali. It's understandable. He is very sorry for your family's loss as well.'

Jackie, a good friend from our young adults' group, arrives, and between her and my mum, they are on the phone to what seems to be every person in the world. I ask Minister Wade to take me to Garth and Merle, realizing I am not able to do it on my own. He drives my car while he gently asks questions about Garth and Merle and their friendship with Cole. I tell him about their lifelong friendship and Cole Jnr getting named after Cole. When the car comes to a standstill outside their house, I freeze, unable to move to open the door.
How am I going to do this? How can I be the bearer of such bad tidings to such wonderful people?

Minister Wade is at the door, and he holds it open with his left hand and presents his right hand to help me out of the car. My legs are shaking so much that I can't walk properly. Putting one foot in front of the other, as I hold tightly to Minister Wade's arm, I walk up the driveway. Like a robot, manually instructing the body how and when to function, I reach the veranda.

'Take it slowly, Tali. I know this is going to be so hard for all of you –'

He has not finished speaking when we are knocking on the front door.

'I can't do this; I can't, I can't! Oh no, please, I can't! How do I even begin to tell them? I can't –' I panic.

Gasping, tears roll down my face before I can stop them.

'Just breathe, Tali, slowly, breathe –'

Again, he doesn't finish his sentence, and the door opens. For an instant, I see the delight on Garth's face when he sees me before he realizes something is amiss.

'Tali, what's up? Hello, sir,' He looks questioningly at Minister Wade as he opens the door wider for us to make our way into the lounge.

'Merle, come here quick!' Garth shouts, and she is by his side in a matter of seconds.

'I am Minister Wade.'

They shake hands as I stand close to Minister Wade, trying to hide my face. I know that if I look at Garth, I will lose control of the very thin, loosely-tied threads that are holding me together right now.

'Tali, what's going on?'

I sense that Merle already knows, and all I can do is shake my head.

'It's, it's…' A deep, desperate sob wells up inside me, and my body heaves with the effort to control it.

I want to burst out into hysterics again, but I need to tell them. I just don't know how.

I see the concern in Garth and Merle's eyes, and Merle reaches for my hand. 'Tali? What happened?'

I look imploringly at Minister Wade, begging him to tell them. I just can't. Thankfully, he understands.

'We have some distressing news to tell you. I think Tali would like me to tell you; she is not capable of doing it right now.'

I nod my head in agreement and continue to cry, tears gushing from my eyes like waterfalls.

'Mr. Medeck and Cole were involved in an accident this morning, just outside of Colesberg. I'm afraid to say that no one survived.'

It is not difficult to feel Minister Wade's pain. That he doesn't want to be doing this is written plainly on his face, but he does it nonetheless. Merle covers her face with her hands as she wails, and tears spurt from her eyes. She exclaims, over and over, that it is not true, that it cannot be true. Garth, Cole's dearly beloved friend, buckles with anguish and releases a heart-wrenching cry. The sound is unbearable, and I cover my ears as I look on numbly. He crumbles to his knees, and he rests his head in his hands. As tears stream through his fingers, he continues to cry.

What can I do to ease his pain? I wonder, but watching his pain only increases mine.

I want to go to him, put my arms around him, and comfort him, but my legs won't let me. Minister Wade reaches for him, but he jumps up and runs out of the door, screaming at the sky.

Oh, poor Garth, oh poor, poor Garth.

Merle gingerly walks down the stairs and onto the lawn. They hold on to each other and cry like babies. I can hear them through the open window. I walk over to the couch and sit down, unable to control my grief, feeling increasingly awful for bringing them this heartbreaking news. Minister Wade stands in the middle of the lounge, unsure what to do or who to console. He looks at me for reassurance, but I am not able to offer him even a comforting glance. I stare at him blankly, my face void of all expression and feeling. He comes and sits down next to me.

'I'm so sorry, Tali, I know it means nothing right now, but I truly am.'

Garth and Merle come back inside, and Minister Wade stands up so they can sit next to me. We embrace one another, trying to find some comfort. After what seems like an eternity, we calm ourselves from hysterics to rolling tears. Minister Wade goes through the details of the accident and offers to make us all some coffee, which we gladly accept. Merle explains where everything is and goes to check on Cole Jnr. She comes back into the lounge with the baby in her arms. She holds him out to me, and I reach to take him. As I look at his pudgy face, his perfect nose, his twinkling eyes, I realize how he will never know his namesake. We will have to make sure he knows of Cole and knows what a wonderful person he was. I think how Cole would have treated him as his own and loved him as his own. These thoughts bring me such sadness again that the hysteria starts threading its way back to the surface. I hold the infant even more tightly, and it becomes the only way I can stop myself from doing what Garth had done: run outside and scream at the sky and ask God why He has let this happen.

Why has this perfect human being been taken from this earth when his life had only just begun?

It doesn't make any sense. It is not what I wanted my life to be. *Why? Why? Why?*

I fight every urge inside of me to stop myself from becoming angry. I know I am looking to blame someone, and if someone does not give me some answers very soon, I know I will blame God forever. Cole Jnr stares at me. His eyes are still not their proper color, but soft and loving – as if he is telling me it will all be okay, don't get angry, be calm, and the answers will come. All I can do is look back at him and cry. I hold him to my chest and feel his small, fragile body in my arms, so dependent on his parents for his existence. A small degree of calm settles in my mind, allowing me to breathe normally again.

'Have you phoned Bob and Jeny?' Garth asks after a long silence.

'Oh, Garth, it was so awful! I couldn't do it! When I heard Bob's voice, I couldn't tell him! So, I gave the phone to Minister Wade, and he had to. They are devastated and are making arrangements to come home immediately.'

'How are your mom and Eric?' Merle's brow furrows with concern.

I snort. 'My mum is incredible! She says she can't mourn when she knows my dad is with God, where he's wanted to be almost his whole life! She says she must rejoice for him! Eric is beside himself, though. I don't think I've been much help to him at all; the way I've reacted.'
'You can't control the way you react! Good grief, Tali, this is a shocker beyond shockers,' Merle says comfortingly.
I give Cole Jnr back to Merle.
'I need to get back to the house, there are still a million awful phone calls to make and things to organize, and it's already so late in the day.'
'Would you like us to come with you?'
'No, but thanks, perhaps tomorrow will be better.'
I look at Minister Wade, 'I'm so sorry, you've been here with us for so long, I'm sure you have other places to be.'
'Goodness, Tali, this is where my place is, please don't apologize.'

After we say goodbye to Garth and Merle at least a dozen times, Minister Wade and I go home. My mum is still making phone calls, and people crowd the house, seemingly wanting to attend to me every second. I feel exhausted, but I know I have to make a few more calls of my own. I politely excuse myself and go into the spare bedroom. Sondra and Cheri are shocked and upset by the news and promise to stop by the house on their way to work in the morning.
Another day with more people, I complain to myself.
All I want to do is be alone and wallow in my sorrow. Tomorrow I will have to try and get hold of those two men, Nick Drummond and Henry Lategan, to let them know too. I will have to phone Cole's boss now, before tomorrow.
Do I have the courage or the energy, I wonder, but I have no choice in the matter.
I have a hard time getting the words out. It is late, and I am tired, and when I start to speak, all I want to do is cry. Naturally, Cole's boss Derek is horrified. He promises to send me the numbers I need in the morning and to relay the news to Cole's colleagues and associates.

Aside from all the calls I make, my cell phone does not stop beeping. Messages flow in fast and furious, making it difficult for me to try to sleep. I put it on charge and switch it off, hoping to get some peace. I crawl under the covers and try to come to terms with this drastic turn of events.

My father. My dear, sweet, kind, loving father who will never hug me again. I'll never get a kiss from him again, nor hear his gentle voice call me "Talia-May."

As I remember his touch and smell, I feel the uncontrollable urge within me to sob. It reaches up from the core of my being, and, bringing my knees up into my chest. I curl into the fetal position and put a pillow over my head. I want to block out the sound escaping from my throat, as my body jerks with every sob. I want to scream to release this pain ravaging my body. The sound of the front door closing and my mum's footsteps on the tiles silence me. I cannot let my mum see or hear me like this. She needs to mourn, too, and to have to be supportive of me will not allow her the chance to do so.

'Talia-May, you asleep, my love?' Her voice is that of a mother truly dedicated to her child's needs, even when hers are in tatters.

I wipe my face with the sheet. 'No Mum, you want to jump into bed with me tonight?'

I clear my throat, and she opens the door quietly, and I lift the duvet for her. She climbs in.

'It's going to be okay, dear, just have faith.' And then her voice cracks.

My super mum is human after all; she knows when to be strong and when to be humble.

'Mum, I don't know, it's so unfair.'

I reach out and put my arms around her. We lie in each other's arms, and finally, she cries. I cannot remember ever seeing my mum cry, except perhaps in a movie.

'He has been my life since I can remember.' Between her sobs, I manage to make out her words, 'Will I be able to carry on by myself? It's going to be so hard without him.'

I hold her tight to me.

'Just cry, Mum, let it out, you need to let it out.'

And so we continue to cry, to sob, to hold each other, to talk, to ask questions, and to cry again, until we have no tears or words left. And then we drift to sleep, holding on to each other for the comfort, the love, and the support that only a mother and a daughter can give each other.

I know that when I switch my cell phone back on, there will be numerous messages, so while I make an effort to get coffee, I wait just a bit longer. Mum is already on the phone, making arrangements for the memorial service on Thursday afternoon at the church. Listening to her, I shudder at the thought of having to arrange Cole's. Just as quickly as I think it, I shrug it off. It is too early to start thinking.

The doorbell chimes, and I automatically look at the clock. It's 08:00, too early for visitors. Mum stands dead still and waves her hands at me, signaling for me to open the door. I do as she asks, not caring how I look at all. With a cup of coffee in one hand, I unlock and open the door. Sondra and Cheri stare back at me, not saying a word. The minute they lay eyes on me, tears collect in their eyes. There is no need for words, only embraces. They've arranged to come in late so they can visit with my mum and me before work.
'Josh was so upset when I phoned this morning. He asked us to relay his and his family's condolences, and he says he'll phone you later in the day. Shame, he sounded genuinely upset, Tali,' Cheri says with difficulty, trying to hold back her tears.

When they leave, I make toast for my mum and me, and as we sit down at the table, I switch on my cell phone. I am right. There are way too many texts and voice messages, so much so that I think about switching it off again, but my mum suggests I deal with them now.
'Get it over with,' she says, and I know she is right.
I listen to the voice messages and read the text messages slowly. The worst message is from Bob and Jeny, letting me know that they will be back by tomorrow afternoon. I can hear the sadness in Bob's voice as he struggles to stay in control. I

put my head in my arms on the table and sob. I was hoping to be stronger than this this morning.

'It's okay, my love.' My mum, my super-mum, is always here for me.

'Mum, I know I'm not supposed to question God, but how or why would He take Cole now? His life was only just beginning; he could've done so much for God here on Earth. I don't understand it!' I speak angrily through my tears.

'It's not for us to understand Talia-May, but for us to accept that God does what is best for us. You know, He will never give us more than we can handle. I know it's hard to accept and understand right now, my dear, but Faith will get you through this. The church and I, we are all here for you. Use us as your support rather than the world, and don't try to get through it all on your own.'

I get up and hug her. I know she is right. I make my way to the shower and to face the day.

CHAPTER TWENTY

People flow in and out of the house all day. Eric assumes a lot of responsibility, making arrangements and handling all the necessary legal paperwork. I still have not touched anything of Cole's.

Soon after 11:00, Garth arrives, and I feel such relief, as though some weight has lifted from my shoulders. At last, there is someone to share my burden with me.
'Can you come with me to Cole's flat, please? I suppose I should look for whatever paperwork there is, if any at all?' I look questioningly at Garth.
'Of course, can we do it now? I think we should.'
We leave for Cole's flat. I'm sure Garth feels as anxious as I do as we approach the apartment building. It feels as if a panic attack is going to strike me at any second, and I hold on to the car door for support.
Garth notices and puts his hand on my arm, and in a calm, steady voice, he says, 'Tali, it has to get done. Let's get through this so we can move on. I'm here, you know you're not alone.'
His positive attitude makes me gather courage, and I take strength from him. 'You're right, let's go.'

Taking the first few steps into his flat, when Garth opens the door to allow me to enter, I take a deep breath. I can still smell Cole here; his scent lingers, even though he hasn't been here for over a week. His presence fills the room. I gasp as I battle to catch my breath, and I sit down on the sofa. I let my hands rub the seat on either side of me as if I can feel him sitting here. Garth leaves me alone while I fight to control my emotions. I don't want to be weak; I want to be able to walk in here, get what I came for, and leave without breaking down. Garth calls to me from the bedroom to make sure I am okay. I get up slowly, my fingers lingering on the couch, and I go to Cole's bedroom. I find Garth sitting on the bed, still made up in the neat way Cole always made it, with a box in his hands. I know that box. It's full of photos and memorabilia from the life we shared. Taking a deep breath, I sit down next to Garth as he begins to open the box with his hands trembling.

'Please close it; I know there aren't any legal documents in there, please, Garth!' I beg him, knowing that if I even see one photo of my smiling Cole, my heart will break.

He snaps the lid shut, and we get up and look through Cole's cupboards and drawers. Eventually, Garth finds what appears to be a Will, along with other documents that look like insurance policies, and we leave immediately. While we drive back, I ask him, 'Do you think having a memorial service for Cole on the beach where he always surfed would be okay?'

Garth sighs and nods his head, 'That will be perfect, Tali. I wanted to suggest it to you. I've got all our mates' numbers and can let them all know. Just let me know when and what time.'

'Thanks, Garth, you're the best. Sorry, I'm putting this on you, I can't do it on my own.'

'Hey Tali, we're all here for you, don't try to do it on your own. That's what that minister dude said, didn't he?'

I smile at the way Garth refers to Minister Wade.

'Thank you; I know you must be hurting so much too.'

'Yeah, it still doesn't seem possible or real yet...' Garth trails off.

'Would it be okay if I came round to your place later this afternoon?'

'When I drop you off, I'm going to fetch Merle, and then we're both coming back to you to spend the day with you. Anything you need, we're with you to handle it.'

'You are both so special, thank you.'

A few tears trickle down my face. Cole always said what a good friend Garth was, and now he is exactly that.

When we arrive at my mum's, Eric, most unusually, greets me with a long, affectionate hug, 'Hey sis, hang in there, okay.'

I do not want to let him go. I hold onto him a little longer and then realize there is a house full of people behind him. Reluctantly, I let him go, kissing him on the cheek as I do.

'So, what are the plans for Dad's memorial? You need me to do anything?' I ask Eric.

'We can talk to Mum later once everyone's left. It's impossible to get her attention right now without getting interrupted.'

Agreeing to talk about it tonight, I escape to the spare room. The box I took from Cole's, I place on the bed. Then I check my cell phone, which I conveniently left at home when we went to Cole's. There are, of course, loads of messages again, and as I start going through them, it rings.

'Hello Tali, it's Josh here. I asked Cheri to relay my family's and my condolences, but I wanted to tell you myself, too. I'm not sure if this is a good time?'

His voice sounds sincere and so full of concern, which touches me, and I'm instantly grateful that he has phoned.

'Hi Josh, thanks for phoning. Now is as good a time as any! Thanks for caring, it means a lot to my family and me, and please thank your family too.'

'Will do. Please let me know if there's anything I can do for you, and please don't even think of coming back to work until you're ready. There's no rush, okay?'

'Josh, that is very kind of you, thank you. I appreciate it so much. I'll email you the details for both memorial services if you'd like to attend.

'Thank you, Tali, yes, we will be there. My father, in particular, would like to attend your father's service; he was very fond of him. Again, Tali, please don't hesitate to ask for anything.'

We say goodbye, and I hang up, still deeply touched by his kindness and concern. I finish going through all my messages, and while doing so, fall asleep. The sound of Garth and Merle arriving with Cole Jnr wakes me up, for which I am grateful, as I do not want to sleep; there is still so much to get done.

I go into the kitchen and make everyone some coffee. Judith starts chatting to Merle about Cole Jnr, since it's the first time they've met, and Eric and Garth throw around suggestions for when it'll be best to hold Cole's memorial. My mum has finally found a few minutes to have a nap.

'Just for half an hour, Talia-May, I want to recharge. There are still lots of things to arrange.'
She has so much energy that I feel inadequate at not being able to handle the situation as well as she does. Suddenly, for some strange reason, I think of the two men Cole was so fond of, Nick Drummond and Henry Lategan. I still have to phone them! On hearing the news, they are devastated, having been the last people to see Cole and my dad alive. It comes as a terrible shock, and they both assure me they will attend both services. It's difficult to tell them, but somehow I manage. Naturally, there are tears from both sides, and at times, I am not even able to speak. But I am not hysterical, nor do I feel an impending anxiety attack; I now know that I can get through this.

After a small meal of macaroni and salad, very generously provided by the ladies of the church, we are alone as a family. It feels unfamiliar, without my father – his presence was always noted, not for being boisterous or dominating, but purely for his gentle manner. We make the final arrangements for his memorial service and arrange with his right-hand man, Clive, to handle GB Tours until we can deal with that.

As for Cole's service, Garth and I agree on the beach service, but we will have to wait for his parents' return before making any final decisions. Although things seem to be moving forward, at the same time, it feels as though time has stood still, and we're meant to be in this state of limbo forever. The worst part is dealing with the undertakers. As kind and comforting as they are, they represent the finality of this nightmare. I know they're just doing their job and that they are a necessity, but I cannot help but take an instant dislike to them. They are taking away from me that which I loved most in this world.

While Eric, my mum, and I are sitting in the lounge – for once not talking, arranging things, or being comforted by a flow of people – in peaceful silence, we are disturbed by the sound of the doorbell. We all let out a sigh and, without speaking, know that the doorbell's sound is unpleasant news. Finally, Eric gets up and unwillingly goes to answer the door. From where I sit, I can see two men standing at the door. My heart sinks, and I begin to tremble.

What now? Surely there can't be more bad news?

It's two police officers, waiting for Eric as he composes himself after the shock of being greeted by them. Eric ushers the two of them into the lounge, but they do not accept his offer to sit down or to have something to drink. They remain standing and slowly make their way to where my mum and I are sitting.

The smaller officer, exceptionally skinny, with big, round glasses – nothing a person imagines an officer to be – has his hat under his arm as he stands rigidly in front of us and begins to speak calmly and precisely.

'We understand this is a very difficult time for you, and please accept our sincerest condolences. This is indeed very tragic. We knew Mr. Medeck well and, therefore, took it upon ourselves to return his and Mr. Mellor's personal belongings to you.'

After the smaller officer says this, we all sigh with relief, and the plump officer goes outside, bringing in familiar suitcases and several other packets salvaged from the accident. Suddenly, it feels like it's starting all over again, as if I'm hearing the news for the first time. A loud gasp escapes me, and I find myself battling to breathe. In between loud, embarrassing gasps, I begin to lose control. With my head buried in my hands, the tears flow, and the more I sob, the more my shoulders shake.

Eric quickly helps the second officer take the bags out of sight to the garage, while my mum chats to the first officer, who is genuinely sorry for our loss. He explains that they knew my dad very well through his business and respected him immensely. After Eric and the second officer return, my mum gives them the details of my dad's memorial service. They promise to be there and leave, once again expressing their sympathies. I do not doubt that they will be there.

It takes me some time to compose myself again. Finally, I resolve to climb into my mum's bed to calm down. Eric and Judith are spending the night, so they will be using the spare room. I grab Cole's box from the spare room and jump into my mum's bed, with the cold metal box clutched between my fingers.

Bob and Jeny are arriving this afternoon. Fortunately, they will use a shuttle service from the airport and come here directly. My stomach has been in a tight knot from the moment I woke up. Another episode I am not looking forward to facing.
If only next week would come and go without me having to wake up or having to deal with any of it at all.

As usual, we gather in the kitchen for an early cup of coffee and some toast, not that any of us feel like eating, but we know we should. Minister Wade will be coming over at about 10:00 to go over all the final arrangements. He has also offered to be here when Bob and Jeny arrive. His support for my family is irreplaceable; he is undoubtedly a guardian angel sent by God. I cannot begin to comprehend how Bob and Jeny are feeling; their anxiety must be so immense. To lose your only child, and to be informed of it while so far away. It is too terrible to imagine. I shudder and decide that a steaming hot shower will be good therapy.

Almost right after my shower, my stomach is in knots again. Like the big ones, they use on ships to anchor them to the port. So much so that wrapping my arms around my stomach seems to hold me together, as though if I let go, I will simply fall apart.
Later in the afternoon, I hear the sound of a vehicle pulling up in the driveway and, getting up from the sofa, I let out a nervous sigh, almost surprised that I don't disintegrate. Mum, Eric, Judith, and Minister Wade get up too, but I reassure them that I will greet Bob and Jeny. It's the right thing to do; I remind myself. I reach the front door and open it gingerly, hoping it's not Bob and Jeny, even though I know it is. They

are taking the last of their luggage from the bus when I approach them. My heart is racing so fast that I can feel the palpitations in my throat and my ears.

What do I say?

'Tali, darling!' Jeny comes towards me; her arms are wide open. There is no need for words as we embrace each other. Jeny cries, I cry, and after a few minutes, Bob, having tipped the driver, embraces us both, tears streaming down his face. Eventually, we compose ourselves and, my fingers firmly around Bob's hand, we go inside, and I introduce them to Minister Wade, Eric, and Judith. My mum embraces them warmly.

Surprisingly, it is not as emotional as I expected. Aside from our initial outbursts, the rest of the time we spend with Bob and Jeny is calm as we explain how the accident happened and discuss the memorial services we've arranged—the details of Cole's service we discuss and finalize with them after a delicious dinner. As I suggested, it will be held on the beach on Saturday at 11:00.

'I can't imagine Cole wanting it any other way,' Bob agrees.

When they say goodbye to Minister Wade, I cannot help but overhear Bob ask if they could meet with him one day, as they have a few questions. Of course, Minister Wade is obliging and sounds only too pleased to help.

CHAPTER TWENTY-ONE

Thursday morning drags on forever. The phone doesn't stop, and people are in and out of the house constantly. Judith offers to go with me to my house to find something decent to wear. I've been living in the few items of clothing I always keep at my parents' house, and they are not suitable for the service. I feel fine, mostly because I do not stop to look at photos or anything else that will remind me of Cole. I dig through my cupboard and grab a blue dress and my favorite black sandals before Judith, and I rush out again.

All I can think of is that I have to stay strong today. I have to get through this service without breaking down. My mum is rejoicing because my father is with Jesus, and I should do the same. My brain keeps telling me it'll be easy, but my heart doesn't agree.

We arrive at the church building early, and already there are more cars parked outside than I've ever seen parked here before. I walk into the entrance hall, and the first thing I notice is a huge portrait of my dad up against the wall. One can't miss it, and it takes my breath away so much so that I stand frozen in front of it. I stare and stare until someone gently holds my arm, supporting me.
'It's okay; I've got you.'
 I try to remember who the gentleman is, but I can't. He was close enough to see my sudden distress, and I am grateful to him for helping me make my way to the foyer, where we get crowded by sympathetic friends, family, and colleagues. My father's business has closed for the day, and the staff is here to attend the service. The kind gentleman is still standing beside me, guarding me.
'Thank you, I'm sorry to be so useless,' I say, finally remembering my manners.

'Please, Ms. Medeck, don't apologize. My name is Reyn, and I'm a deacon here. If there is anything I can help you with, please don't be shy to ask.'

'Thank you very much,' I manage a smile, 'the kindness of everyone has been so overwhelming, I can't imagine ever being able to return it.'

'It's not to be paid back, Ms. Medeck. Your father was the most honorable man I've ever known. He was always my inspiration. What an example he was to everyone around him. But now we can celebrate that he is with Jesus.'

I look at him.

He is so confident, just like my mother.

I nod and walk away.

Minister Wade informs us that it's time for us to take our places in the auditorium for the service to begin. A sense of calm washes over me as the service opens with a welcome message and a prayer. Then, one by one, people stand up to pay their respects to my dad. Each person who speaks shares the most touching thoughts and memories of my father and declares how he will remain in their hearts forever. What is incredible to me is that no one cries; they only rejoice. At times, it is too surreal, and I grimace. I have never experienced anything like this before. My mum, sitting between Eric and me, is radiant. She does not look like a widow mourning the loss of her husband; she looks more like a bride. Each person silently acknowledges us as they walk past. Eric and I nod, and my mother moves her lips to say a wordless 'thank you.'

I cannot be upset now, how can I?

For the duration of the service, even during Minister Wade's incredible sermon, which moves me to the splinters of my soul, I feel uplifted, not beaten down. I rejoice alongside these people, who loved and respected my father so much, hopeful and without sorrow. What affirmation! The choir gathers on stage and sings as though angels themselves have descended from Heaven. They pay homage to my father and glorify God. The music sends shivers down my spine as I hear every syllable that pours from their hearts, so full of meaning. A tear rolls down my cheek, and I don't brush it away, completely and utterly moved by this service conducted in honest Christian love, for a man I will always love, and, one day, will hopefully be with again.

Snacks and refreshments are served in the building after the service so we can thank each person for their kindness, prayers, and for making the effort to be here. Amongst these wonderful people are Nick Drummond and Henry Lategan. I tell them over and over again how grateful I am for the influence they had in Cole's salvation. Eventually, I introduce them to my mum, and as I stand alone in a sea of people, lost in thought, I feel someone lightly touch my arm.

'Miss Medeck, I got you a cup of coffee. Thought you could do with a cup by now.'

I turn around, and my heart swells, 'Oh, Booker, how lovely of you to be here, thank you for being so thoughtful, I'm so thirsty!'

Relieving him of the cup, I hug him with my other arm. It's a strange emotion that overcomes me as he puts his arms around me – as though I need him here, and it's comforting to know that he is.

'It was a wonderful service, Miss Medeck, nothing like I have ever been to before.'

'Yes, definitely, but it was so perfect for my father, I can't imagine anything else would have sufficed. I'm so grateful it wasn't very sad; I wouldn't have been able to handle that.'

'The other ladies from your office are here, and so are Mr. Josh and Mr. De Luca. They are standing over there.'

I look to where Booker is pointing and give a sigh of relief when I see my faithful friends and the De Lucases standing a few strides away. Without hesitation, we walk over to them. Sondra comes towards me, her arms outstretched. She embraces me warmly, as does Cheri. It's difficult to hold back the tears, but they are gentle tears, and my friends wipe them away tenderly.

Mr. De Luca extends his hand, and when I shake his, he covers our hands with his other hand and never takes his eyes off mine.

'I'm so very sorry, my dear, your father; he was a good man. If you need anything at all, please ask. I will be leaving now. Thank you for inviting me to the ceremony. Your father will be smiling in Heaven, I'm sure. God bless you.'

With that, he releases our hands, says a few words to Josh in Italian, greets Booker, nods at Sondra and Cheri, and before I can blink, he is gone. I'm still standing amazed and appreciative of his little speech when Josh puts his hands on my shoulders.

'I'm so sorry, Tali, you know I liked your dad, he was one of the best and won't be forgotten, not after this ceremony.'

Josh looks at me with just the hint of a smile, which makes me smile in return.

'Thank you, Josh, it's good of you to come.'

We all keep chatting for a while until I notice Garth and Merle looking lost. I excuse myself and invite them to join the 'work crowd.' After introducing everyone, we continue chatting – Merle and Cheri talking babies, and Josh and Garth deep in conversation.

Who wouldn't want to chat to Garth? I ask myself.

Sondra, Booker, and I keep each other company. Eric and Judith join our group as well, and, pulling up some chairs, we remain in the corner of the room until the afternoon turns into evening. I am sure my conversation is no longer making sense to anyone. I am so tired, yet no one seems to want to leave. There isn't even any food or beverages left, and still, no one leaves. Booker, dear, sweet, considerate Booker gently mentions to everyone that I look exhausted and perhaps they should think of heading home. Slowly, the room empties of all these wonderful people who care so unselfishly for my family and me.

At 22:00, my mum, Eric, Judith, and I stumble into my mum's house and go straight to bed.

CHAPTER TWENTY-TWO

It's Friday, and I'm spending the day with Bob, Jeny, Garth, Merle, and Minister Wade. We are finalizing Cole's memorial service at Bob and Jeny's house. I thought they would be so much more emotional than they are. Even at my dad's service, they were composed; saddened and somber, but nothing like I expected. Their quiet acceptance of their son's passing is a little unnerving for me, and when I had a moment with Minister Wade at my dad's service, I mentioned it to him. He told me he visited with them on their request the night before. He said he explained the Truth to them, what it meant to Cole, and that he is in Heaven now. He said they questioned their salvation and where they might end up one day. I only stared at him as he told me, not expecting this at all.

He smiled, 'Don't look so shocked, Tali, you know God works in amazing and mysterious ways.'

'Will they be studying with you some more?' I asked.

'They said they want to wait until after Cole's memorial, have a bit of time to mourn, and then they would like to very much.'

I was speechless if Cole's death means another two souls will get to Heaven, then it is meant to be.

Knowing today will be difficult and horribly emotional, I wish I could go back to sleep and never wake up, or else skip past today without knowing it existed. Either one will not happen as my mum unfortunately already has the kettle boiling and toast ready.

'Morning, dear, you okay?'

'Thanks, Mum, I don't know how I feel, but I don't want today to happen.'

'It'll be over soon enough; the day will go by quickly, you'll see.' She tries to reassure me.

'Did you know that Bob and Jeny visited with Minister Wade, and they want to study further with him?' I still sound so surprised.

'Just goes to show you, love, God works in ways we will never understand.'

'That's what Minister Wade said too.'

My cell phone rings. It is Garth sending me a message:

The angels and Cole will be smiling on us 2day as the weather is going to be perfect the whole day.

I tell my mum, and we giggle a little, knowing it is probably true.

After a long, hot shower and cleaning up the house for my mum – it seems as though a hurricane has gone through it in the last few days – I leave for my house.

Do I still have a house? It probably needs some cleaning too. I'm sure some of the guests and family will visit after the service, and I also need clean clothes!

The intercom buzzer sounds. It's probably Garth and Merle to fetch me. I've changed into Cole's favorite outfit – three-quarter denim pants, a green T-shirt, and flat brown sandals. I quickly press the intercom to allow them in, gather up the huge photo Judith had done of him, and grab my sunglasses. As I check that I have enough tissues, Garth takes the stand for the photo to the car.

Standing next to the car, I look at Cole's surfboard on the roof racks. A lump rises in my throat, and I look unseeing, mesmerized, until Merle puts her arm around me.

'It's so hard now, Tali; it's hard for all of us, but if we can get through today, it will get better in time. I'm here for you, don't forget it.'

'Where is Cole Jnr?' I reply, feeling the need to hold him.

'He's sleeping in the car.'

I get into the car and sit next to him, not saying a word. I hold his hand as he sleeps peacefully, so unaware of what is going on today. I have to fight back the tears and the urge to cry.

It will not do me any good to break down now; I keep saying to myself as we drive to the beach in silence.

When we arrive at the beach, we offload the car and take our time walking to where the ceremony will take place. Minister

Wade, Jackie, and a few of our friends from church are already waiting for us at the water's edge. Minister Wade will lead the ceremony, say a few words about Cole, and give our thanks to everyone for coming. No eulogies will be given, but we've requested that people write a note to Cole's parents to treasure. We've provided paper, pens, and a special box that Jeny has had since Cole was a baby. Minister Wade approaches us and greets us warmly. He assures me that it will be a ceremony befitting Cole's character.

'I'm afraid I won't be able to handle it,' I splutter, 'what if I'm not strong enough?'

I clutch Cole Jnr as though my life depends on him. I'm afraid that if I let him go, I will fall apart, that if I let go, I will have nothing left – that my heart will crumble, and I will fragment into grains of sand and washed away by the lapping waves.

'Tali, don't worry, we're all here for you. Have faith, put your trust in God, and it will be okay.'

There's no more time to dwell on my sentiments. Cole's parents arrive, and again their composure astounds me. It will be easier, I am certain, to get through the day with their kind of attitude, and soon enough, there are dozens of seemingly calm and smiling people at our little spot on the beach. I notice Nick Drummond and Henry Lategan and go over to greet them warmly.

'Thank you so much for coming; Cole was so very fond of both of you. He's in Heaven today partly because of you,' I remind them once again.

'God will lead us; all we have to do is plant the seed, and if nurtured, it will flourish.'

'I would very much like to chat with you both a little longer. I hope you won't leave immediately after the ceremony.

'No dear, we'll be here for a while, that sounds wonderful.' Nick smiles.

My mum joins us, and I leave them chatting once again, as though they've been friends forever. I find Cole's parents and bring them over to introduce them to Nick and Henry, too. I secretly hope they will have the same influence on Bob and Jeny as they did on Cole.

'Tali, Minister Wade says we should start; everyone seems to be here.' Garth comes up to me and takes my hand.
He leads me to the water's edge. Merle, Bob, and Jeny follow and stand close to me.

Minister Wade calls out to everyone that we would like to start with the ceremony, and everyone gathers around us, at the edge of the ocean. The sea is calm and very flat, with no waves to speak of at all.
As I look out over the sea, I wonder if Cole ordered this perfect day for this occasion, and I smile wanly.
Minister Wade reminds everyone to write a message to Cole's parents and explains that after a short message from him, Cole's best friend, Garth, and his other surfing friends will take his ashes out to sea and lay him to rest. I've asked Garth to put his ashes into the metal tin Cole kept all our photos. Minister Wade keeps his message short, simple, and very touching. He compliments Cole for the man that he was. Tears are not required, but smiles, in memory of my dear Cole.

The surfers gather at the edge of the ocean, the sea washing over their bare feet. They hold their boards as Garth goes in first, the metal tin that holds my world balancing on the tip of his board. I stare as one by one they paddle out on their boards.
How many are there? I wonder and count.
Forty-eight, wow, forty-eight of our surfing community are here today to pay tribute to Cole.
My heart swells, and the tears flow. I cannot help it; this sincere expression of friendship and love moves me. I take Cole Jnr from Merle again and hold him tightly, kissing his forehead.
'This is so perfect for Cole, Tali, I know he is enjoying watching this, I know he is.' Jeny says and puts her arm around me, and leaves it there while we watch Garth sit up on his board.
The other surfers do the same. They gather close together, forming a huddled group, bow their heads, and on the shore, we can hear the murmur of a farewell prayer. Garth opens the tin, lifts it high up into the air, tilts it, and as a slight breeze

blows gently, Cole's ashes fly up into the sky. I watch them dance in the wind, then sink into the water, into nothingness. Cole flies from my life but not from my heart. I gasp and try to catch my breath as I overcome my anguish. Merle cries too, and Jeny holds me tightly. I hang on to Cole Jnr for dear life. Bob turns around and embraces Jeny and me, his calm composure broken.

Singing reaches our ears – it is our friends from church. They sing, 'God be with you till we meet again,' and soon everyone joins in. Bob, Jeny, and I remain as we are for a little while longer and then lift our heads and look to the horizon. Garth comes out of the ocean first, and as he hits the sand, he drops his board and the metal tin and runs straight to Merle, flinging his arms around her. I seem to have, while wrapped up in my emotions, forgotten that Garth has also lost his best friend, his brother, his lifelong buddy. He is hurting so much, too, and has been nothing but everyone's pillar of strength. I feel so bad, so selfish, far too wrapped up in myself when here I can see Cole's best friend hurting just as much as I am. He is too good a person to let me worry about his pain. As 'Amazing Grace' is sung, I embrace Garth and Merle. Garth is distraught. After days of holding back, he releases all his pain. He sobs so much that his shoulders shake violently, and a sound of anguish erupts from his throat.
Poor Garth, poor beautiful, gentle, loving Garth.

Somehow, we manage to compose ourselves, and the rest of the afternoon we spend talking about Cole, and we get to know others we have not met before. I make a particular point of thanking every surfer for helping to make this tribute to Cole so perfect, and I'm not surprised to find how much every one of them loved and respected Cole. As I chat with them, I realize how much they are like him; each with a love for life and all things simple – like Cole, there is nothing false about them.
'Tali, you are amazing. For someone who has had to go through this twice in one week, you are truly an inspiration.'

Josh, Sondra, Neville, Cheri, Tian, and Booker come over to hug me and to express their condolences. They all comment on how perfect this ceremony was for Cole.

'It's only thanks to all the support I've had that I've been able to get through it,' I reply to Josh, once I've greeted everyone.

He takes a step forward and hugs me for the first time. Not even at my father's service did he do it. It feels natural, as though I were hugging a friend.

He is a friend, is he not?

The weather is still perfect, although a slight wind has picked up. Minister Wade asks everyone to turn and look at the sunset. The sky is still a bright blue, interrupted here and there with a few puffy clouds that have gathered to say farewell to Cole as well. The sun is a fiery red ball, sitting on the horizon. It still shines so brightly that it is difficult to look at without sunglasses.

'I would like to ask you all to raise your glasses or paper cups, and toast a man that was – a gentleman, a man of God, a loving son and a loving fiancé. As the sun sets on this perfect day that God has graced us with, we celebrate and pay tribute to Cole. We can all take this opportunity to thank God for allowing this wonderful man, Cole, to be a part of our lives, even if for so short a time. I've spoken to almost everyone here today, and the love you have for Cole is a testament to the person he was. He will always be a part of our lives and will always be remembered as perfect as the sunset. He's an angel with God in Heaven now, guarding over those he loved most.'

'Here, here,' resounds from the guests, and then we fall silent as we watch the sun set on this perfect day and Cole.

I bow my head and pray as the tears fall gently down my cheeks. Cole is gone, but he will live on in my heart forever and never be forgotten.

CHAPTER TWENTY-THREE

The weeks seem to fly by quickly. Some days are easy, and others, as expected, are more difficult to get through than I could ever have imagined. Most nights, I fall asleep with my arms wrapped around my abdomen, seemingly holding my body together. I drift off crying and wondering whether this pain and emptiness will ever go away, or even just ease up a little.

Garth, Merle, Eric, and Judith kindly helped me pack up Cole's flat. All the things no one wanted to keep, which weren't much, as he didn't have much, were given to the church for benevolence. Garth took most of his clothes, and I've kept some of his jerseys to sleep in.

My father's and Cole's Wills and Testaments were read and sorted out easily enough. Eric and I get the business, but neither of us is inclined to carry on with it. My mum gets the house and everything else, plus enough money so that she need never worry about money ever again.

To my surprise, Cole left me as the beneficiary of his pension. He, unknown to me, had taken out a life insurance policy naming me as the beneficiary. He also left an insurance policy for Cole Jnr, which will continue to run until he turns twenty-one. This comes as a huge surprise to Garth, Merle, and me, but then again, we all have to agree it's typical of Cole: always considerate of others.

The magazine company he worked for reclaimed his 4x4, so there's not much else to do other than wake up every day, remember to breathe, and slowly start living again. Life will go on, very differently from before, but it will nevertheless. I know I have a support group in my family, my friends, and the church, but most of all, I know I must rely on God.

I stand in front of the elevator. It has been over a month since I last wondered which elevator would win.

Number One today, I think to myself with a British accent, and it is Number One that arrives.

'You know what's good for you,' I murmur as the doors open.

I walk in, and, turning around, I notice Booker watching me like a mother hen. I'm sure I'll get a lot of this for the first week or so, but I don't mind, it is, after all, what good friends do.

I'm the first to arrive at the office, and I go about my usual routine, not forgotten by my weeks of absence. While I wait for the coffee to brew, I stare out the window at the clear, bright day, hinting that spring is in the air. I start to wonder what Eric and I will do with the business. Neither of us is interested in running it, and as much as Clive would love to buy it, he's told us he will never be able to raise the capital. Soon, my mind wanders into nothingness, and I stare blankly through the window. I don't even notice when Sondra and Cheri walk in until Cheri touches my arm.

'Hey, hello, you okay? You don't have to be here; De Luca said you could take as long as you wanted.'

'Oh hi, yeah, I know, but I'd rather be here than alone at home.'

'Coffee?' Sondra has already poured me a cup and has a warm croissant ready.

Some things never change, and I feel strangely grateful for this small mercy.

'Besides, I can't even begin to imagine the work I have to catch up on; it'll be just the distraction I need.'

'We did as much as we could; you'll find little post-its all over the show!' Cheri chuckles as she points to my desk, and, looking carefully, I notice piles of papers with little pink, purple, and yellow bits sticking out all over.

We all laugh, chat for a short while longer, and then make our way to our desks. There is so much work to catch up on that the days fly past. Most nights, I take work home, and that helps me get through the long, lonely hours once the sun has set. Everyone at Rio Adventures is incredible, respecting my space and situation while allowing life to carry on as usual. Brett and Greg are grateful to have me back, and never hesitate to harass me over trivial issues.

During a busy afternoon at month-end, my work almost up to date, a Skype message from Josh pops up on my screen. My heart sinks as I read the message:
Please come to our office.
My mind swirls with reasons as to why they want to see me. I've tried my best to get up to date and to get on with life as best as possible. There have been very few occasions when I've cried or felt depressed at work, and they wouldn't know about any of them.
Do they think I'm not coping? Are they going to fire me? I wonder frantically. On and on my mind wrestles as I walk slowly towards De Luca's office. Once there, I hesitate at the door, sigh, and knock.
'Come in,' sounds from the other side.
Gingerly, I open the door and first notice De Luca sitting behind the desk and then Josh standing by the window. Nervously, I walk in.
'Please, Tali, have a seat.'De Luca stands up and motions to the chair in front of the desk, his voice kind and friendly.
Maybe I'm not in trouble after all.
'Thank you,' I say, so quietly that I don't think they hear me.
'How are you, Tali? Are you coping, getting through each day okay?' Josh speaks for the first time, his voice filled with concern.
'It's difficult, but I'm coping and getting through it, thank you for asking,' I reply as I look down at my hands and at the engagement ring that shines ever so brightly.
'Tali, you must know that we're aware your father's business got left to you and Eric,' De Luca hesitates before continuing.
He seems to be waiting for a response from me, so I oblige him, 'Yes, it is common knowledge.'
'I want to ask you – what do you want to do? Do you want to quit here and take over there, or do you have other plans? Have you and Eric even thought about it seriously yet? I know it's very soon, but you can't leave something like this for too long.'

'We've discussed it at great length, but we're not sure what to do. Neither of us wants to run it, and we will be meeting with our lawyer on Saturday.' As I answer, I try to figure out where this conversation is going.

I realize they're probably concerned that I might resign and that they'll have to find a replacement, though there seems to be something else they want to discuss.

'So, you would sell?' Josh asks.

'Yes, that's why we want to speak to our lawyer. We don't know what a respectable asking price would be, or even how to go about it.'

'Can I speak frankly?' De Luca asks.

'I thought that's what we are doing?' I answer.

Josh laughs, and De Luca smiles.

'Would you mind if we put in an offer for the business? Preferably, I would like to merge the two companies. De Luca hesitates again, opening his mouth to speak, then closing it.

'Oh, well, um, I'm sure it's a possibility. Do you mind if I discuss it with our lawyer first and get back to you?' I'm a bit thrown; this is not at all what I expected coming into this meeting.

'Of course, Tali, we would not want it any other way,' De Luca sounds very positive suddenly, 'I'm sure we can do something that will benefit everyone.'

I leave the office in a daze.

This might be the solution Eric and I have been looking for.

I grin and whisper, 'Thank you, Lord.'

As soon as I get back to my desk, I grab my cell phone and dash outside to phone my brother. As I expected, he is keen to make a deal and agrees that it will be an easy answer.

Back in the office, Cheri and Sondra are very curious about what is going on, so I put them out of their misery.

'Wow, imagine that! It would certainly be a good option to consider,' Sondra nods.

'Eric and I will discuss it with my mum tonight. He's going to phone the lawyer now and fill him in, and then we can decide on Saturday. I hope this will go smoothly and quickly, so we can get this behind us too.'

'We all hope so too, Tali,' is Cheri's kind reply.

As we sit around the table at dinner, my mum intently listens as I recall the conversation with the De Lucases.

As she raises a mug of tea to her mouth, she says, 'I would like to see the companies merge, at least in a small way, then, we'll still have an interest in GB Tours.'

'How do you see that working, Mum?' Eric sounds as confused as I am.

'Well, one of you would have to remain a member.'

'But we don't want to, Mum!' I retort, and Eric echoes me.

She remains quiet and says that we can make further decisions once we've seen Reuben on Saturday. We change the subject and discuss more mundane things. My mum tells us about her support group at church that is doing amazing things with the rehabilitation homes in the area. Eric and I listen, impressed, as she tells us all about their work. I'm keen to get involved.

'I have so much time on my hands now, Mum, I might like to get involved too, so when you go to your next meeting, I'll go with you if that's okay?'

'Of course, dear, that would be wonderful.'

My mum chats happily with us for the rest of the evening. She is coping as we knew she would; she has God on her side.

CHAPTER TWENTY-FOUR

Eric and I wait in the reception area of Reuben's attorney's firm. Our appointment is scheduled for 09:00, and we arrived at 08:45. It's now 09:15. The phone rings, and after a brief conversation, the receptionist puts the receiver down and clears her throat. Eric and I watch her stand up and walk over to us.

'Mr. Breed just phoned and asked me to offer his sincerest apologies, but he will not be able to make the appointment. He has a family emergency to attend to, and has asked that we reschedule.'

There is not a thing we can do about it, so we make an appointment for Monday at 17:30. I am frustrated and don't feel like company. I go straight home and crawl on my sofa bed, where I sleep on and off for the rest of the weekend, with the TV blaring. I weigh up all the pros and cons of the scenarios offered by De Luca, and my mind is frustratingly active whenever I'm not asleep.

In between a nap and some popcorn, it suddenly becomes clear to me why my mum wants someone to remain a member and why she thinks a merger will be the better option. She is concerned about the staff who might lose their jobs.

Why did she not just say so? I frown at the realization.

Immediately, I phone Eric to tell him, and he says he has to admit he thinks I'm right.

'Then we should ask Reuben if we can somehow ensure the staff keep their jobs should they want to! Whichever option he thinks is best. Trust Mum to be concerned for everyone,' Eric says.

We chat about this and that, and nothing in particular, and then say goodbye. I am alone again. The hollow in my chest starts to ache.

What I wouldn't do to have Cole here next to me right now.

The tears roll down my cheeks, and before I can control myself, I am sobbing and yelling at the walls, blaming them because I am alone.

I thought I was over this stage, but clearly not.
I am cross with myself, but the silence, the huge void in my house, consumes me.
Will I ever get used to this hole of nothingness in my heart?
Somewhere between a sob and a tear, I manage to fall asleep.

Eric and I are back in Reuben's reception area. A door to our left opens, and a grey-haired, very short, overweight man stands in the doorway and greets us with a thin smile.
'Hello Eric, Tali, please come in.'
As we enter Reuben's office, he closes the door behind him and apologizes for Saturday's cancellation.
'Please sit, can I get you anything to drink?'
We both ask for coffee and take our seats. We chat for a few minutes about how we are coping with the accident, how my mum is, how his business is going, and how his family is doing until the coffee arrives and we pour.

Saying his office is huge is a mere understatement. I could fit my house in it. There are shelves and shelves of books and tables swamped with files. I wonder how on earth he knows where anything is. It's a very light office, though, not like the ones you see in movies – all dark and dingy. He has photos of his family all over the walls that make me feel more at ease.

I tell him about the meeting with the De Lucases and the different scenarios facing us, as well as our concern about the staff's jobs. Eric interrupts to tell Reuben how we feel about being members of the business. Reuben listens and makes notes continuously. By the time we have finished explaining, almost three pages are covered in his spidery handwriting.
'Do you have financials and asset registers so that I can get an assessment done of the business?' Reuben asks, making more notes.
He looks too short for his desk, and I long to giggle.
'We can get everything from the auditors; I know my dad kept his books very much up to date,' Eric answers, 'or would you rather ask for it? We can give you the contact details.'

'Yes, let me do all of that, then I will have my finger on the pulse, so to speak.'
After two exhausting hours, Eric and I finally emerge from his office. Our minds are more confused than ever, and we are even more undecided, but there is nothing we can do until Reuben has evaluated all the information from the auditors.

The next day, as soon as I am at my computer, I send Josh an email immediately:
Met with the lawyer, he will do assessments; we will meet again. As soon as I have, I will let you know. Hope this is okay with you and Mr. De Luca?
I don't expect a reply because I know he is out of the office all day, but soon after lunch, he replies from his Blackberry:
That is fine, must do it the right way or not at all. Thank you for letting me know. Have a good day.
After I read his message, I read it aloud to Sondra and Cheri.
'He's always so polite to you,' Cheri remarks.
'He's probably just being kind and considering my circumstances.'
'No, I don't think so! He's always been exceptionally nice to you.'

A memo comes through on my computer, and when I read it, my heart sinks. I look up to find Cheri and Sondra staring at me. The invitations to the staff Christmas party on the seventh of December have just been sent out. I do not want to go; that is for sure.
'Everyone will take their partners, and I'll be like a spare wheel with nothing to say to anyone, and I also don't want anyone's sympathy at the party either,' I say defiantly.
'Tali, you know it won't be like that,' Cheri says, already too sympathetic for my liking.
I don't answer her and immediately email to say that I will not be attending.

Once again, Eric and I are at Reuben's reception office waiting to meet with him. As usual, he comes out of the office to greet us. There seem to be even more files than the last time we were here.

Is that even possible?

The same routine follows – he orders coffee, we chat about our personal lives until the coffee arrives and is poured, and then we get down to business.

'Your father kept a very well-run ship. I was pleased to discover. The company shares, which now belong to both of you equally, are R750,000.00.'

I nearly drop my cup, and Eric's mouth gapes in astonishment. The room is dead quiet for a minute or two until Reuben starts laughing.

'I wish I had filmed this moment to capture your expressions right now. They are priceless!'

It's still a few moments before I manage to say anything.

'Really? I can't believe it!'

Reuben goes into great detail, explaining the various options we have and how they will affect us. I listen, although not much sinks in. Fortunately, though, he has drawn up copies of all his assessments and suggestions so that we can take the time to go through them properly and make the best decision for everyone concerned.

Leaving his office, Eric and I go straight to my mum's and explain everything to her. When we tell her what the business is worth, she sits back in her chair and pats her chest, repeatedly fanning herself with Reuben's papers.

'Goodness me, goodness me,' she repeats.

I know how she feels. I knew my father was a good businessman and a generous man, but it never occurred to me that his business was so lucrative. I know for a fact, and so does Eric, that we could never maintain his standard. We discuss it further with my mum and reach the consensus that we will merge with Rio Adventures, on the condition that they keep the staff if they choose to stay after the merger. Somehow, we knew this was the best solution all along, but we had to go through all the motions to convince ourselves we were doing the right thing.

'We will allow ourselves time to pray and to ask God for direction and closure before going to the De Lucases with our final decision,' my mum says firmly.

In the morning, I send a Skype message to Josh as soon as I get the chance:
Hello, we met with the lawyer last night and had a good meeting; please give us time to pray for God's guidance to make sure we make the right decision.
During the morning, I receive a polite reply from Josh as usual:
Of course, Tali, please do not feel pressured into making any decisions you will later regret.

CHAPTER TWENTY-FIVE

The young adults' group and the youth are organizing an "oldies' evening" for all the older members of the church, as well as those at the nearby old-age home. I need to be involved in something to fill the empty hours, and being in God's house gives me a sense of peace, a way to use my time, and a chance to be amongst friends. It is so good to walk into the function hall and have everyone come up to me and greet me with hugs and smiles. I feel wanted.

Tonight, while we discuss themes, games, and ideas, we laugh a lot. I sometimes laugh hysterically for what seems like forever. I laugh till my sides hurt, and it is painfully satisfying. I volunteer to be in charge of the décor, and by the time I get home, I am so exhausted and excited at the same time that falling asleep is easy.

There are two weeks left until the "oldies' evening," and I still have so much to do. At lunchtime, I make my way down to the local bric-a-brac store and find loads of old rock and roll records. Elated, I buy them all, thinking how fantastic they will look all over the walls. Then I make my way to the stationery store to buy thick pieces of board for cardboard figurines to adorn the walls. By the time I'm back at the office, I'm half an hour late. I apologize profusely to Sondra and Cheri, who laugh at me and tell me Josh phoned for me. Wondering why he wants to speak to me, I sit at my desk and dial his extension.
He answers, 'Giosia, hello.'
'Hi Josh, it's Tali. I got a message that you were looking for me?'
'Oh, hello, Tali, yes, I just wanted to ask if you would reconsider your RSVP to the Christmas party. I understand your reasons, and if you feel you would rather not go, then that's okay, but I thought I'd ask.'
How does he even know of my reply?

Pausing before I reply, I say, 'Okay, I'll think about it. You can change it to a "maybe."'

'Thanks, Tali, I'm not pressuring you, but it would be great if everyone attended.'

It's not like I am the heart and soul of any party; in fact, at the moment, I'm the exact opposite, so my presence will hardly get noticed.

Of course, Sondra and Cheri wait in anxious anticipation, dying to know the context of the phone call. When I tell them, they simply shrug and say, "I told you so," and that no one will treat me differently at the party, so I might as well come.

I'm not ready to do this, I keep telling myself, *but maybe after the "oldies' evening" I will feel more up to it. I hope so.*

Every night for the next few days, Eric, Judith, my mum, and I get together after work to pray for guidance. We spend about an hour together and then go our separate ways. Except, of course, on Thursday, when we still have dinner with my mum, and she still cooks up a storm.

There is so much to do for the "oldies' evening" décor. It occupies me almost every evening of the week – except on Wednesday when I go to the young adults' meeting at the church building, and of course on Thursday when my mum cooks dinner.

Excitement at the young adults' meeting grows rapidly for the "oldies' evening." Everyone is helping one another, laughing and sharing as they do. I feel I need to be here with all the other young adults. Maybe it is selfish of me, but I need to be here. Minister Wade is always so supportive and possibly even more excited than the rest of us. I wait until everyone has left so that I can speak to him.

'Do you mind if I discuss something with you? I know it's late.'

'Of course, that's fine, Tali.'

I explain the business concerns and how I feel I am getting directed in one way by God, but do not want to misconstrue my feelings as God's Will.

'Wow, Tali, who would've thought? I'm pleased to hear that you have put your burdens in God's hands; it's so easy to make a decision and take it from there. Sometimes, that gut feeling we have is what God wants us to do. If you all feel the same way, without any reasonable doubt, then I believe that is what you should do. If God wanted you to make another decision, you would doubt in your mind.'

'Yes, that's what I believe! I just wanted to hear that I am going about it the right way. Tomorrow I will speak to Eric and my mum; we need to finalize this once and for all and move on.'

Eric joins me in my office at 10:00. It's Friday, and our meeting with the De Lucases is at 10:30. Sondra and Cheri are becoming increasingly curious because I haven't told them about our final decision. I thought it would be best to wait until everything is signed and sealed before I tell anyone. I make Eric coffee, and before long, it's 10:25. We head to the De Lucas' office, and when I knock on the door, a familiar, 'Come in' greets us.

We go in and sit down – De Luca behind his desk and Josh standing at the window, just like the previous meeting.

Déjà vu, I think, and stifle a giggle.

I briefly admire the fantastic view before becoming a little nervous about whether I should open the discussion or let De Luca. I needn't have worried because De Luca breaks the silence.

'Josh tells me you've discussed and considered our offers and that you have made a decision.' He looks at Eric as if Eric has all the answers, and I'm just here for the sake of it.

I can feel my face growing hot, and then he looks at me, 'Tali, the floor is yours.'

My heart begins to race, and I shift in my chair. I sit up straight and clear my throat, trying my best to act calm and professional and to appear as though I know what I am saying.

'Thank you, Mr. De Luca. We want the companies to merge. But, on one condition – that the staff from GB Tours keep their jobs if they want to, neither of us wishes to be a shareholder or director; we would prefer that our shares be paid out to us.' I take a deep breath, 'I'm sure there are many finer details to consider, and honestly, Eric and I don't know a lot about all of this, so, if you are willing to go this way, we would be much happier if our lawyer handled things from here.'

I can feel my hands sweating, and I grasp them together on my legs to hide their shaking.

'We thought this would be the route you'd prefer and commend you for it. It is the option we prefer as well. Well, it looks like we will be able to make this happen.'

He claps his hands together and smiles at us, as though already celebrating.

'I take it your lawyer has the share values and all the necessary information, so we will speak directly to him from here on.' De Luca continues to smile and extends his hand to Eric, and then me.

Josh moves from the window for the first time and shakes our hands too. I presume the meeting is over and indicate to Eric that we can leave. De Luca does not attempt to stop us, so we head for the door.

'You can email your lawyer's details to me, thanks, Tali,' Josh says, as he walks us to the elevator.

'Oh yes, sorry,' I reach into my bag for Reuben's business card and hand it to him. 'Will you contact him or should I get him to contact you?'

Eric presses the elevator button.

'I've got his details now, so I'll get hold of him, thank you, Eric, Tali, and I am very sure this will work out for everyone concerned. You needn't sit in on all the meetings, but when we notify GB Tours' staff of the merger, we'll most likely have individual meetings with each staff member. It will be good if one of you is present at those.'

The elevator arrives, and Eric walks in, holding the door open for me.

'That will be okay, I'm sure we can do that,' I say as I step into the elevator.

Josh gives us a slight wave, smiles, and heads back to his office.

In unison, Eric and I let out a great breath of air as the doors close. Suddenly, Eric burst out laughing.

'This is brilliant; I didn't notice them earlier!' He laughs even more, 'I've never seen anything like it, ever. Wow, who on earth is the genius that came up with this idea?'

'You'll never guess,' I say as I rub my imaginary 'good work' badge.

'You're kidding, Tali? It's brilliant; it is excellent! You should do this for a living; you'll be famous!'

'Really? I mentioned it to Josh one day. I was nervous about being alone with him in the elevator. He liked the idea, and here it is!'

'Honestly, Tali, it's brilliant.'

'Thanks, Eric, glad you like it. I remember how Cole laughed when I told him.'

Saying Cole's name brings a lump to my throat. I put my head down and fight to keep the tears at bay. Eric puts his arm around me.

'Like it? I love it, Tali, and I'm serious about you doing this professionally.'

'Have you thought about what you're going to do when you get your shares, by the way? Cole left me all that money and now the shares too. I've no idea what to do.'

'Best would be to speak to Reuben, but you should go on a holiday first and then decide what you want to do.'

The doors open, and we walk out into the foyer. Booker opens the huge entrance doors for us and greets us with his warm smile. Eric shakes Booker's hand and thanks him.

'Yes, I also thought it would be best to speak to him. But what's the point of going on holiday if you don't have anyone to go with?'

Again, I fight against the tears welling in my eyes and the lump sitting in my throat. My heart aches even just at the sound or thought of Cole's name.

'It's hard, Tali, I know, but it will be okay. I love you, remember that, hey.'

Dear sweet Eric, Judith is so lucky; he is one in a million.

'I love you too,' I say as I hug him and kiss him before he leaves.

Walking back into the office, and not in any mood to work, I slump into my chair.

'You ladies feel like going out for lunch? I need to tell you what's happening before you both explode,' I say with a laugh.

'We thought you were never going to tell us! We're dying here. Where should we go?' Cheri has already started packing up her work.

'There's a new coffee shop in the mall, apparently; we can try that out?' Sondra, eager too, packs up her work.

I laugh at them, 'You two are both so funny, packing up in such a hurry!'

'Tali, you've no idea how we've guessed these past few weeks. You are very nasty keeping us in the dark like this,' Cheri laughs and looks a little foolish for being so overeager.

Sondra does not bother to hide her feelings, 'You are cruel! Come, we must go now; I can't take the suspense any longer!'

We are all laughing as we leave the office.

The new coffee shop is delightful, very homey and comfortable. The waitress is pleasant, and the food is excellent. As we eat, I tell them about the merger, the shares, and everything that has happened between Reuben and the De Lucases so far. They listen in silence as I ramble on about the first meeting, our evening prayers, our concerns about the staff, and, of course, our shock at the company's value.

'Wow, really, that is huge!' Cheri exclaims once I sit back in my chair.

Sondra looks astonished, 'Good grief, you're joking? Really?'

'What will you do when it is paid out?' Cheri asks, sipping her latte.

'Oh, I don't know yet. You know, Cole also left me a lot of money in a policy I didn't even know about.'

They both stare at me for a few seconds.

'Tali, really?' Sondra looks at me in surprise again.

'I know, I don't know what to do with the money yet. When all the dealings are over, I will ask Reuben for some advice. Eric suggested I go on a holiday before I decide anything, but I told him I'm not keen on going alone. It won't be much fun, you know, and will probably make me more depressed.'

'Yes, you need to speak to Reuben, but don't just speak to him, get other opinions too, then make up your mind. Why don't you take your mum with you?' Cheri says, finishing her latte and calling the waitress. It's already over an hour, but today it doesn't bother me if I'm late or not; my mind is just too active with all the distractions.

'Oh goodness, please not my mum! I love her dearly, but she will not enjoy it at all; she likes her routine and her friends. She has no desire to see the world. She has all she wants to see right here. Oh, I don't know what to do! I suppose the best is if I wait until I have the money and then make up my mind.'

We finish lunch and keep throwing options around in the car on the way back to work. Even back at the office, the conversation continues around the merger of the two companies.

'How do you think they're going to fit all the staff into this building? Will they still use both offices?' Speculating about so many scenarios keeps us from getting any work done until it is time to go home. I hadn't thought of all the implications of the merger.

'I'm sure the De Lucases have considered all this already,' I say, sounding hopeful.

CHAPTER TWENTY-SIX

As the older members and their guests arrive in their rock-and-roll outfits, they are welcomed by some of the young adults. They walk on the red carpet to the function hall on the right of the church. The rest of us are buzzing around with excitement, making some final touches here and there.

I am wearing a pair of tight black jeans rolled up to just below my knees, a red T-shirt, a white scarf around my neck, and red stilettos, which I'm sure I'll regret wearing by the end of the evening.

The venue hall looks amazing. My life-size figures of rock and roll legends are all over the walls, along with guitars some members donated. The records I found are placed randomly on tables, stuck to the walls, and some scattered on the floor.

Minister Wade beams as he ushers the guests to their allocated tables. The oldest lady in our church, Aunty Debs, arrives, and we all clap and whistle and cheer as she walks down the red carpet, just like a movie star. It's such a special moment. Her walk takes some time, as expected, with a frail body at ninety-one, but what an inspiration she is to us all as we watch her enjoy her moment of fame.

My mum and her group of friends arrive. Stunned, I clap louder than before. I have never seen my mother dressed up for any occasion other than church, and she looks fantastic – at least twenty years younger, too! I laugh loudly and hug her as she reaches me at the entrance, and she laughs contagiously.
'Oh Mum, you look fantastic! I can't believe this is you!' I cannot stop laughing as she poses in front of me, twirling her wide green skirt.
With the skirt, she is wearing a broad black belt, a white T-shirt, white socks with a green frill at the top, and white pumps. She has a green-and-white polka-dot scarf tied like an Alice

band in her hair. Short as she is, this outfit makes her look even shorter, but it does not matter; she looks amazing, and I tell her so again. She laughs, her eyes sparkling with excitement and joy.

'Oh my dear, I have not done this in so many years, I'm having so much fun, thank you, love.'

Minister Wade has to drag her away from me and usher her and her friends to their table; they hurry off like excited little girls.

Once everyone is seated, all of us young adults stand against the back wall as Minister Wade welcomes everyone and thanks us for our hard work. The guests give us a hearty applause, and then he says a prayer to bless the food. The guests are treated to a decadent four-course meal, and later, when we clear the tables, we notice there is no food left. Every morsel of food is consumed. Everyone has comments and jokes about these little old people who eat so much, and it all adds to the jovial atmosphere that weaves its web among the people.

No sooner have the plates been removed than the band, teenagers from the youth group, pound a few beats, and the floor in the center of the hall fills with elderly people dancing their hearts out. Jackie and I stand together, thoroughly appreciating every second of watching them having the time of their lives. One song after another is belted out, and very well too, I might add, to the appreciative dancing guests, my mum included. My mum and her friends dance together in a group, her dancing skills reminding me of our private dancing parties when we were younger. When the band stops to take a break, the old people complain so much that the poor boys have to carry on, Minister Wade making sure they are well supplied with water. These elderly people seem to have much, much more energy than all of us young adults put together.

I sit with the other young adults, on chairs we found in a back room, and we laugh together and enjoy this fantastic evening. Every so often, one of the young ladies is convinced to dance with an elderly gentleman. This has the rest of us in stitches as we laugh and make fun of them as they try to keep up with an energetic gentleman. All the games we intended to play are shelved, as all the oldies want to do is dance, and no amount of persuading can change their minds. Dance is all they are interested in, so dancing it will be. For a small moment, just for a few seconds, I imagine how much Cole and my father would have enjoyed this.

Jackie squeezes my hand, 'I bet they're laughing themselves silly watching us.'

I have to agree with a smile.

It is 03:00 in the morning when the hall is finally cleaned up. I took my shoes off long ago, and also put on a looser pair of jeans.

I start my car and say goodbye to Minister Wade, 'See you on Sunday; I'm sure it is going to be very interesting!'

He laughs and waves goodbye. I'm exhausted, so much so that once I get home, all I do is collapse on my sofa bed. I remain there until Saturday evening when I wake up smiling, for the first time since the accident.

CHAPTER TWENTY-SEVEN

Tourist season has arrived, which means the office is increasingly busy and I have to attend numerous meetings regarding the merger. Swamped with work that never seems to get done, it irritates me, as I'm usually always up to date, even at the worst of times. During most of the merger meetings, I am lost in translation within the first 15 minutes. There are endless papers to sign, and every time Eric and I look to Reuben for assurance.

A Skype message from Josh pops up on my screen:
Good morning Tali, Saturday is the Christmas party. Have you given any more thought to attending?
I groan. Sondra, who is standing behind me, starts laughing.
'Oh come, Tali, look how much you enjoyed the oldies' thing.'
'I hardly think this party falls into the same category.' I argue.
'Gosh, he is ever so polite,' Cheri says, now also behind me, reading the message over my shoulder.
Good morning, I will attend, but please excuse me if I don't stay very long.
'Yay!' Cheri exclaims, and both she and Sondra return to their desks happy with my decision.
Thank you, Tali. We do appreciate this; of course, that is acceptable. I read his reply to both ladies; they repeat it in unison with posh accents, and we all laugh.
'I don't have anything to wear, will you help me, come shopping with me, if you have time?' I ask them rather sheepishly.
Fashion is not my forte.
'Ooh, shopping! Most definitely! ' I will find any excuse to go shopping,' Cheri replies immediately. 'It's this Saturday, Tali. We can go this afternoon! Sneak off work a bit early and then if you don't find anything you can always borrow something of mine.'
'Oh yes, Cheri, like I am ever going to fit into your clothes.'

'Tali, have you not noticed how much weight you've lost?' Cheri asks me, more out of concern than mockery.

I look down at the way my favorite black three-quarter pants fold loosely around my thighs, and I realize for the first time that I have become incredibly thin.

'Yeah, suppose I have,'

We go into every shop there is, but cannot find anything worth buying. Perhaps it's because I do not want to go to the Christmas party. We go to Cheri's house to see if she has something I can borrow.

'This is ridiculous; I don't even want to go to the stupid party,' I complain while I look through drawers and shelves of Cheri's clothes.

She has enough to open her own boutique.

'Wow, Cheri, you do have enough clothes!'

'I can't help myself! I see something I like, and it bugs me until I buy it! Luckily, I have a son and not a daughter, more money to spend on me!' she says, shrugging her shoulders and smiling.

I try on one dress after another, eventually losing count of how many I've tried on. After at least twenty, I get bored, flop onto the bed, and look around her room; clothes are everywhere. Sondra is having a great time, acting like a movie star and making us laugh, but I've had enough of putting clothes on and off.

'I think the red one you haven't tried on yet will fit the best, Tali,' Cheri takes a very dark red dress down from behind the door.

I drag myself up, try it on, and have to admit it fits perfectly.

'Okay, I'll take it. Can we please stop now?' I say, making sure I sound tired and not ungrateful. 'I can't see why I have to bother; I'm only going to be there for two hours.'

Hesitantly, I ask, 'Would you mind if I get ready at one of your houses? I know I won't do it by myself; I got ready at Jackie's for the oldies' party.'

'Oh Tali, of course, you can get ready here, it is so understandable, please don't think we all don't know how hard this is for you, we do, really we do. But we also know it is not good for you to be on your own, alone all the time. A bit of a distraction is healthy!' Cheri sits down next to me on the bed and picks up my hand and pats it.

'I suppose you're right, thanks so much,' I cannot say another word, the same old lump begins to swell in my throat.

The tears well and roll down past my ears.

Wiping them away, I sit up, 'Sorry.'

I get off the bed and start cleaning up. Cheri and Sondra don't say anything further, join me in cleaning up, and when I leave with the dress and a pair of dark silver heels, they hug me tightly.

CHAPTER TWENTY-EIGHT

The sun is shining, and there is not a breath of wind in the air. It is a perfect day, a day to be outside. The past few weeks at work have been exhausting and confusing, and today's weather provides some much-needed relaxation for my body and mind. As usual, being alone is not a good way to achieve this. The Christmas party is tonight, but I still have many hours to get through until then. While I have my morning coffee, I dial Garth and Merle's number, hoping to spend the day with them. It's been a while since I've seen them.

While Garth surfs, Merle, Cole Jnr, and I relax on the beach and enjoy the glorious day. It's the place where we said goodbye to Cole, and my heart lurches.

'Garth is battling Tali, I know you are too, but almost every night I hear him crying in the lounge. He doesn't show it much, but he's having such a rough time, so I was pleased when you phoned this morning. It's as though you're his only connection to Cole. After the accident, he would pick up photos of Cole and stare at them for ages. Sorry, I probably shouldn't be telling you this; you have so much more to deal with in your life. It's just that I'm so grateful you called.' Merle speaks slowly, choosing her words carefully in an effort not to upset me.

'No, I'm glad you've told me, Merle. Sometimes I think I must be the most selfish person in the world; I'm so concerned with my loss, I forget that others are also suffering. Poor Garth, we don't realize that men love their friends just like we women do. I mean, Cole was like a brother to him. Does he talk about Cole at all?'

'Tali, no one could ever accuse you of being selfish, don't ever think that! He doesn't speak to anyone about it, not even to me. I'm very worried about him; he can't keep himself so bottled up, it's not in his nature, and one day he's going to explode, I know it.'

We play with Cole Jnr in the sand and watch Garth surf – the waves are enormous, and he surfs as though he is demon-possessed and fighting for a title. I tell Merle about the young adults' group at church and how much they've helped me, especially by involving me in the oldies' party, and how they allow themselves to be shoulders to cry on without hesitation.

'Do you think Garth might be interested in joining us one evening? He probably has so many questions he cannot find answers to; if I did not have my faith, I would be as lost as he is now.'

'I honestly cannot tell you how he would react. He is such a closed book right now.'

My heart aches, Garth is hurting, and I have failed to support him.

How can I help him?

'I will speak to Minister Wade at church tomorrow, for advice on the best way to approach this.'

'Thanks, Tali, we can work on him together, just let me know what I must do.'

There is a strong tug at my heart.

Is this a door opening for me to save the souls of my precious friends?

The wind picks up, and Cole Jnr starts getting tired. Garth is finally surfed out, and I have to get ready for the Christmas party. Reluctantly, I say goodbye, promising Merle I will speak to Minister Wade about Garth, and then I get into my car and go directly to Cheri's house.

Once I've had a shower, which is wonderfully refreshing after being in the hot sun and beach sand all day, Cheri decides how to do my hair. If I had it my way, it would just be left to dry naturally, but Cheri has other ideas. She straightens it, then curls it, then piles it up on my head with delicate strands hanging down my neck. I put on the dress and shoes, apply my usual basic makeup, and then put on the earrings Cole gave me. I have not worn them since Sondra's wedding, and although they are green, they go well with the dress.

I stare at the mirror, 'Cole would say to me now, "Wow, love you look stunning," I miss him so much, Cheri.' She embraces me and strokes my back.

The urge to cry is so strong I have to fight hard not to, then, as if ordered, little Tian comes running into the room wearing his dad's shoes and tie. We can't help but laugh, gladly letting the sadness escape the moment.

Once Sondra and Neville arrive, we all leave in our cars and make the forty-five-minute trip to LeRue lodge. The function room is situated at the back of the lodge, away from the main building, and is fairly large, with a thatched roof and massive beams that add to the rustic atmosphere. The décor is mostly made up of pieces that, to me, look like sculpted driftwood, eagerly admired by everyone entering the room. The massive glass doors, spanning the length of either side of the room, fold open to let in the fresh evening air, creating an ambiance of a camp-out rather than a party. The chairs are big tree stumps with a gold cushion on each seat.

De Luca stands up, makes his way to the DJ, and, upon being given the microphone, begins to address us. Silence falls very quickly as we listen to his speech. He says a very short thank-you to everyone for attending, and wishes everyone a wonderful festive season and a great time tonight. Then he gives everyone something to think and talk about for the rest of the evening.

'As of Monday,' he says, 'very exciting things are going to be happening, don't worry, no one is leaving but …' He hesitates, 'Oh, you can all wait until Monday,' he says, chuckles and hands the microphone back to the DJ.

There is silence as everyone tries to figure out what De Luca is saying. Sondra, Cheri, and I look at each other. I have sworn them to secrecy, not even allowing them to tell Neville or Tian. Now there is a buzz among all the guests, growing louder and louder as De Luca sits down with a smile on his face. Josh does not seem very happy and speaks sternly to his father. As I watch him, I notice for the first time that he has a date. She looks like a supermodel, tall and skinny with long blonde hair, and, according to my standards, is wearing way too much makeup.

'Hey, Josh brought a date,' I whisper to Cheri and Sondra, who instantly look his way. Josh and his date become our topic of conversation until the food arrives. Even Neville and Tian join in on our little gossip session, as we've never seen him with a date before, and we've always wondered what taste he has in women. Now we know and look disapprovingly in his direction.

The food is disappointing – typical catered food of roast meat with a few vegetables, salad, and a trifle for dessert. Tian and Neville complain bitterly about how little is served, and when Tian goes for a second helping, the food is finished. He and Neville discuss whether a nearby restaurant might still be open. Our plates disappear from the tables, and the DJ's sounds take over from the constant sound of voices and laughter. Then there is the sound of moving feet, and in the next minute, the dance floor is full of people. I take this as my cue to leave. I noticed long ago, almost from my time of arrival, that I am the only single person here, and I have no desire to sit and watch everyone else dance. I say my goodbyes and leave, sure that the De Lucases didn't notice me at any rate, so if I don't say goodbye to them, it won't matter. I know this is in bad taste and very impolite, but I slip away, justifying it to myself by thinking that I will apologize on Monday.

Monday, I do not want to think about Monday now.

CHAPTER TWENTY-NINE

The entire staff of Rio Adventures is crammed into the conference room waiting for De Luca. Josh waits by the window, staring out like he usually does. I wonder what he is thinking. I am sitting next to the chair that he will occupy, much to my objection, but De Luca insisted, and who am I to argue?

'Thank you all for coming,' De Luca begins as he enters the room. Everyone hurries to sit, including Josh, and he continues. 'As you all know, Tali lost her father not too long ago,' he looks at me, 'well, we have merged with Mr. Medeck's company as of last week. No one will lose their jobs or anything like that; you might, in fact, get a bit busier! We will be holding individual meetings with each of you throughout the week, so please think about any questions or concerns you might have, and we can discuss them then. A memo will go out today with your appointment dates and times; please let us know immediately with a valid reason if you are unable to make your slot. Thank you. That will be all.'

He starts to leave, seems to change his mind, turns around and says, 'And if I find out that any of you has been bothering Tali about this matter, you will be in trouble.'

It looks like he wants to say something else, but instead, he walks out.

Josh stands up, 'Things will be as normal, and business will carry on like it does every other day, we will just have another division now, and you will see more faces around here. No one needs to panic; we just wanted you to hear it from us before the rumors start making their rounds.'

He picks up his file, 'Tali, please come to the office, thank you,' he says, loud enough for me to hear and soft enough for no one else to.

Then he leaves, too, and a hushed murmur begins to move through the room, slowly getting louder and louder. Everyone looks confused. I quickly leave with Cheri and Sondra and feel very grateful I confided in them earlier. While they make their way back to our office, I make my way to De Luca's.

'Come in,' sounds from inside. I go in and am not surprised to find Josh staring out the window and De Luca behind his desk. I can paint this picture from memory by now.

'Tali, how are you doing?'

I reply after a moment, 'I have my moments, but otherwise, I'm okay, thanks.'

I keep my reply short, sure that De Luca wants to rush through this meeting, as he does with every meeting.

'It takes time, dear.' Again, he takes me by surprise, his voice so gentle and filled with compassion.

It seems he feels we are on a personal level, not just a professional one. Of course, I do not mind; it just makes me a little nervous.

'We will be meeting with the employees of your father's company this afternoon. Please, will you be present?'

I nod as he continues. 'When we start with the individual meetings with them, we would like you to sit in on those too. There is no need for you to get involved with the meetings here.'

I am so relieved that he does not refer to my father as "your late father"; the constant reminder would be terribly upsetting.

'How is your workload at the moment?' Josh asks.

'I'm a little busy, nothing unmanageable, though.' I answer, turning to look at him.

'Well, if it gets too much and you feel you need help, especially over the course of the meetings, please ask, and we will make a plan for you.'

'Thank you,' I reply as I stand up, presuming the meeting is over. 'Oh, sorry, what time is the meeting this afternoon?'

'At 14:00, you can drive with us if you like?' Josh replies.

'No, I'll be fine, thank you. Should Eric be there too?'

'If he wishes, but it's not necessary, your lawyer is going to be there,' again Josh replies.

'Oh, okay, I will speak to him, although I am sure he would rather not be there.'

'It will all be over soon, dear,' De Luca says, kindly and fatherly once more.

'Thank you, Mr. De Luca, I am just so very grateful we could make this happen. It has been a blessing to my family and me.'
I leave, but Josh is hot on my heels.
'You left the party so early!' He accuses me.
'I'm sorry, I didn't think anyone would notice if I disappeared.'
'Of course, we noticed, but we also understood.'
'I should have said goodbye; I apologize for that, it was rude of me. When everyone started to dance, I knew being the only person there without a partner would upset me, so I thought it better to leave.'
'No need to apologize, Tali, but why do you say you were the only person there without a partner?'
'I was.'
Wasn't it obvious to everyone?
'No, you weren't, I didn't have a date either.'
Surprised, I hesitate and, not being able to help the surprised tone in my voice, I say, 'Then who was the lady with you all night?'
'Ah, you see, if you'd stayed longer, you would've found out that the lady in question is Carena, my cousin. She is visiting from Canada for a few weeks.'
Oops. We will have to take back what we said about him.
'Again, Josh, I'm sorry I left without saying goodbye.'
'It's okay, Tali. You did tell me you wouldn't stay long. I would've just liked a dance with you.'
The elevator arrives, much to my relief, as I do not know what to say next. We get into the elevator, and as I see the doors, I am reminded of Eric's reaction to the cartoon.
'My brother loves the cartoons on the doors; he couldn't stop laughing at them.' I smile at the memory of Eric's enjoyment. 'He says I should do it as a career.'
'He's probably right! I've never seen another elevator anywhere in the world like it,' he smiles back.
He does have a lovely smile; I think to myself as I feel my cheeks color.
We say goodbye, and I stroll into my office.
'Well, ladies, hope you're all ready to repent?' I grin, 'The blonde we all assumed was Josh's date is, in fact, his cousin!'
I don't know why, but somehow I'm relieved.

CHAPTER THIRTY

Reuben meets me outside in the parking lot, sensing this will be difficult for me, and he is right. I see photos of my father on just about every wall with different celebrities or staff members, and it sends a sharp pain through my chest. Automatically, my arms fold around my stomach so that I don't fall apart. Reuben puts his arm around my waist – he is too short to reach my shoulders – and walks at my pace through the corridors.

Entering the conference room is like walking onto a stage for my first-ever live show, with everyone's eyes fixed on Reuben and me. Josh comes over to us, shakes Reuben's hand, and shows us to our seats. Reuben shakes De Luca's hand and sits down after making sure I am comfortable in the seat next to him. De Luca opens the meeting by giving everyone the news, assuring them of their jobs, and informing them that individual meetings will take place from tomorrow.
No one seems surprised or remotely upset, and I get the feeling that Clive gave them a heads-up.

By 15:30, I am back in my office and relieved at the way the meeting went. There were a few questions some of the staff had, but nothing serious. I settle into my work again, but it's difficult to concentrate with the constant interruptions, either from meetings or from Cheri and Sondra's continuous flow of questions. When my phone rings, I groan as I pick up the receiver, 'Tali speaking, hello.'
'Tali, can you come up to the office, please?' It's Josh.
I put my head in my hands.
'I wish this were all over and done with!' I close the files on my computer and stand.
'Who wants you now?' Sondra asks sympathetically.
'Who do you think? The De Lucas, of course!' I reply, annoyed.

Once more, I knock on the door.

'Come in.' The reply and the same scene plays out in front of me – De Luca behind his desk and Josh staring out of the window. I sit down in the same chair in front of De Luca's desk.

'Tali, with regards to your position at the company – we have a proposition for you.'

Just like De Luca, straight to the point.

'We feel that Mrs. Schoeman will be able to cope with both companies' work, and we would like to offer you a better position within the company.' He pauses, giving me time to absorb what he has just said.

I try, but this is far from what I expected, and besides, I do not know anything beyond accounting.

'We would like to offer you a position with us,' he gestures to Josh, 'the title, I suppose, is "executive PA" but it will be much more than that. Not running around after us but working with us, alongside us.' He pauses again, but I do not notice, 'You are the only person we feel we can trust, and Mrs. Logey wants to retire at the end of December, which means we will have to get someone in her place in any case. Also, you have impressed us so much with the way you handle situations, and this is the quality in a person that we are looking for.' This is where he stopped talking, I think.

'Take a breath, Tali.' I feel a hand on my shoulder that makes me jump back into reality.

'You okay?' Josh speaks for the first time.

'Yes. I am, I think, I don't know what to say, I don't know anything except accounting. How will I know what to do?'

'Naturally, you don't have to give us an answer now, and we can speak more about what your position will involve. We understand this will be new to you, but we know you'll be able to handle it.' Josh answers for De Luca.

'How long before you need an answer?'

'Well, let's say that we want to give everyone a month to settle into their new surroundings, so you can take this month to make up your mind.'

'Thank you; I don't know what to say, the truth is, you've caught me by complete surprise.'

'Yes, we thought that might happen!' De Luca seems to find it very amusing and replies with a smile.

As I leave their office, I am confused, surprised, and more undecided than I have ever been in my entire life. All I want is my bed. Decisions can be made later. I text Minister Wade to ask if I can discuss it with him after church on Sunday, and, of course, he obliges.

Sleep welcomes me tonight as I hold onto the photo of Cole – as has become my habit since the accident – and as I drift off, I pray to God for guidance in yet another decision I have to make.

'How long do you have to make this decision?' Minister Wade asks after I explain the offer.

'Until the end of December,' I reply, as we sit comfortably on the back steps of the church building.

Minister Wade finds that for some reason, people open up much more on these steps than anywhere else.

'You know that in a few months from now you will be getting quite a lot of money, so why don't you go on a trip somewhere? Take some time off, and then make up your mind. You probably have some leave due to you?'

'I've thought of that, but I cannot see that helping me. Going away on my own will only make me more miserable, and I doubt I'll make the right decisions in that frame of mind.'

'Which brings me to the point I want to make, Tali – staying in the same position you're in now will become mundane. Taking on a new challenge like this will keep your mind busy, and I'm sure it'll entail quite a lot of overtime. Also, you'll probably be out of the office a lot. My point, Tali, is that it's something new, and it sounds like it could help you heal. I hope you can understand what I mean.'

'Yes, I do, and you make a lot of sense. The past few weeks have been busy because of all the meetings, but once they're over, it will be back to normal. Get up, go to work, go home. It leaves too much time for my mind to think of how much I miss Cole and my dad. I know I need to move on, but it's also still so soon for me.'

'Of course, it is, and no one expects anything else from you; you have to heal in your own time. But you're in a comfort zone, and I think you're more than this, Tali. I've seen it in you. No matter what I say, though, it's your decision. Let's pray together and ask God to guide you.'

We kneel, and he holds my hands in his as we bow our heads. He asks God to help me, to show me, and guide me to make the right decision, and whatever I decide, that I may emit God's glory and compassion.

When we finish praying, Minister Wade walks with me to my car, and as I'm about to get in, he looks at me sheepishly.

'I need some advice from you…' He trails off.

I look at him and nod my head, 'Anything.'

'It's Jackie. I want to ask her out for coffee, do you think she will say yes?'

I thought by now I could not be surprised by the unexpected, but I'm so surprised that I cannot suppress a giggle as I tug on his arm.

'Really, this is wonderful. I had no idea! Well, I never notice these things at the best of times. You should ask her. She often talks about you, and now I know why.'

He blushes. It is the first time I've ever seen him blush – even the old ladies that flirt with him don't get it right. It's lovely, and I am happy for him and very sure Jackie will accept in a heartbeat.

Cheri and Sondra are horrified at the thought of my leaving the office and try to find every reason in the book to justify my staying, although they know the change will do me good. I appreciate how much they care for me and, as much as this office has become a security blanket for me, I know a move to something new will be the best thing for me right now. It's not as though I'm moving away. My friendship with them is strong enough to handle being separated by one floor, of that we are all very sure. Everyone else, my mum, Eric, Judith, Garth, Merle, and Jackie, agrees that the new position will do me a world of good.

The last meeting slot is deliberately kept for Mrs. Schoeman because what they tell her depends on my decision. I make up my mind after days and weeks of exhausting every argument, and, as it turns out, there are not many arguments on the con side. I pray all the time and am positive this is what God wants for me. I know He must have a plan for me, a plan for why Cole's life ended so soon. It has to be for a good purpose.

The morning after I make my decision, I send Josh a message on Skype:
Good morning, is it possible to meet with you and Mr. De Luca sometime today? Thank you.
It's three hours later when his reply arrives:
Sorry for only getting back to you now, let's make it 3 pm.
My stomach twists itself into at least a hundred knots.
'Oh goodness, oh, I pray I am doing the right thing,' I repeat to myself over and over as I make my way to De Luca's office just before 15:00.
'Come in.' The same voice and the same scene greet me as I enter the office, and I sit down before being invited to do so.
My hands begin to sweat, and my mind races, suddenly thinking about the negatives and that maybe, just maybe, they do not want me anymore.
'Tali, you wanted to see us?' De Luca snaps me out of my thoughts.
'Um,' I clear my throat, 'the position you offered me a few weeks ago, um, are you still of the same opinion to have me?'
I've already forgotten what I've said as soon as I say it.
Why on earth am I so nervous?
Josh turns from the window and looks at me, 'Of course! We have been waiting for you as we said we would. Have you made up your mind?'
'Oh, um, sorry I kept you waiting, I did not mean to take so long, um, yes, I would like to take you up on your offer.'
Not knowing what else to say, I remain silent. They can lead the conversation from here. De Luca jumps out of his chair and comes to stand next to me.
'This is good news, Tali, good news. I have a really good feeling about this. Welcome to the top floor.'

He extends his hand to shake mine and smiles at me. My heart pounds and aches, for at that moment, that smile is a father's smile, and I desperately long for it to be my father's smile.

'We have one more day of meetings, and then we will speak to Mrs. Schoeman. It is too busy right now to make drastic changes, so if you can show her, obviously, depending on her decision, your work and setup, then, shall we say, as of the first of February, you will start up here.'

De Luca seems to have it all worked out. He probably knew I would accept.

'We are going to change things up here and make you a temporary office for now. We are planning to add onto this building so we can move everything over here, but that will take some time, so, until then, it will be organized chaos but still workable.'

'Thank you for this opportunity, I hope I won't disappoint you,' I say and walk to the door.

'I know you won't disappoint us, Tali. You will enjoy it, I'm sure.' Josh puts his hand on my shoulder, a notion that has slowly become a habit, as I step out of the office. Now there is no turning back.

CHAPTER THIRTY-ONE

Days, weeks, and months flew by, and with them the festive days – Christmas, New Year, and Easter. I am immensely lonely during the festive season, missing Cole and my dad so much that the emptiness consumes me. Even being surrounded by family and friends does not ease the pain that wrenches my heart into strips and then wrings them out to dry as barren bits of nothing. But with the sour comes the sweet, as I rejoice in the baptism of Cole's parents just before Easter. Garth and Merle join the young adults' group and seem to be enjoying studying the Gospel with Minister Wade. Cole Jnr develops a gentle and happy character. These are the little things that make my self-pity and misery bearable.

While I get more and more comfortable in my new position at work, the De Lucases get more involved in the new wing being built for the new division. There have been no major hiccups or obstacles; everyone simply gets on with what needs to get done. Cheri, Sondra, and I still have lunch together whenever possible, and I make frequent visits to their office. Mrs. Schoeman – Gina, fits in as if she's been there forever – a coffee lover and a real chatterbox. She is forty years old and married with two teenage children. She has very short blonde hair and happy features, and she, Sondra, and Cheri get on like a house on fire. So, life goes on day by day. Almost a year has passed since the accident, but sometimes it feels like it was only yesterday.

My office is temporarily next to the De Lucas' offices, and to accommodate this, the boardroom has been divided in half. The new boardroom will be in the new wing, which will be an extension of this floor. The existing building is just getting extended to the left and should be completed within the next month or so. It couldn't come any sooner, as the dust and banging mean an overflow of headaches and long faces. The only one that is unchanging is dear Booker, always a smile, always pleasant, and always a gentleman.

On my way up to the office after some much-needed grocery shopping, Greg stops me in the foyer.

'Please, can you pop into our office for a few minutes?'

Some things will never change, I think to myself.

'Okay, let me just put these things in the office fridge, and I'll come down to you,' I say as I continue walking towards the elevator.

Greg walks with me but does not offer to help carry a bag.

And he wonders why he is still single!

He gets off on his floor, and it's not much longer before I make my way to their office. June, Brett, Greg, and Suzie from Rio, and Tray and Zelda from my father's company are all looking at a huge board.

Yep, some things never change.

'What's up?' I ask, and they all turn around to look at me.

Greg speaks first, 'This is an advert that will go up on the billboard by the mall, what do you think?'

I stare at the poster – an Overlander full of people, laughing and pointing at the Big Five standing under a tree. Some people are skydiving in the background, and others are canoeing on a river to the left of the poster. A tour bus from my father's company, coming up from the rear, with similar smiling people on it. It is impressive and their best work yet.

'I like it,' I say.

There is a sigh of relief as they all sound out, 'Yes.'

'Why is my opinion so important? It's not like I'm an expert, to me if a picture is funny I normally like it, other than that I'm useless!'

'Ah, you know us, Tali, your opinion has always meant something to us, and besides, you know the De Lucas better than any of us do, so we reckon if you like it then they probably will too.' Brett grins.

'Don't count on that. I have no idea what the De Lucases are thinking most of the time. They have their way of doing things, and I've known them for as long as you have!'

'Well, do you think they will like it, it is within the specs they gave us?' June asks, still staring at the board.

'I'm sure they will,' I say, and leave them agreeing that they did a great job.

I smile to myself. It feels good to know that someone still needs me and that my opinion still counts for something. I was worried that working on the top floor would give the friends I have worked with for so long the impression that I'm unapproachable or too important to still just be me.

Josh greets me as I walk out of the elevator.

'Hello Tali, just the person I want to speak to,' he offers his usual polite, gentle smile.

'Have I done something wrong?' I reply immediately and reveal my biggest inner fear - that I cannot cope with my new position. That I will disappoint the De Lucases, who have so much faith in me for some unknown reason.

Josh giggles, 'Why would you have done anything wrong? Is there something I should know about hmmm?' He teases me, and I cannot help but laugh.

'Sorry, I just always feel that I am going to make some huge mistake at some point.'

'Well, we'll deal with that if it ever happens, but I doubt it ever will. You're doing great!'

'Thanks, Josh,' I reply, and wait for him to tell me what he wants, but he walks me to my office in silence.

'The new wing will get finished in two weeks, so we want to have a small celebration to welcome GB Tours. Everyone has just got thrown into the mix with it being the busy season, so we haven't welcomed them – nothing formal or too fancy, though.'

'Okay, well, I don't like formal or fancy, so it shouldn't be too hard for me.'

He sits down on the small sofa next to my desk as we continue to discuss the event. It's so easy to talk to him, and I find myself wondering why I was so afraid of him for so long. After discussing the event for quite a while, Josh changes the subject.

'How are you otherwise, Tali? Not to drag up the negative, but it's been nearly a year since the accident. Are you doing okay?'

'I think I'm okay, I have a terrific support group at church and a few close friends, and with my family, it's not often that I'm alone for long. Thank you for asking.'

'I can't imagine what you've been through, and I admire the way you've come through it.'

'It all comes down to my faith; if I did not have faith in God that I have and the support from the church…' I trail off. 'Well, I just can't think what I would've done.'

'Someday you need to tell me more about this faith that you have.'

'Anytime,' I reply, and while we are in this friendly zone, I take the opportunity to ask Josh for some advice.

'Can I ask you for some advice, please, if you have some time?'

'Please do, I have plenty of time today, which seems a bit strange considering the past few months of chaos.' He smiles and gestures with both hands for me to speak.

'Well, you know I've got a bit of money from Cole and of course, the shares, well, the thing is, that I don't know what to do with it. I'm not arrogant, please don't get me wrong, but there have been so many suggestions as to what I should do that now I'm more confused than ever!'

He opens the file he always carries with him, takes out an A4 page, closes the file, rests the paper on top of it, and clicks his pen.

'Let's go through all the suggestions and list all the pros and cons of each.'

As he writes down every suggestion I can remember being given, I make my way to the sofa and sit down next to him. It is easier to talk when I can see what he's writing.

'Is there anything you want to do, like go on a holiday, or is there something you want to buy? Let's deal with that first.'

'I know our church needs a new bus and my mum, Eric, and I are thinking of buying one together. Eric says he knows of a secondhand one in immaculate condition, going for a good price. Also, they've recently started a small orphanage, so I would like to help there.'

'Okay, and what about buying a house?'

'I suppose I should. It would be a good investment. I'd like to get something close to the beach that has a flat for my mum. I was surprised when I asked her that she said she'd like to. The nights are awful for both of us.'

I sigh when I think of how lonely the nights get, and thoughtfully, Josh quickly speaks before I can dwell on the thought for too long.

'Have you spoken to Reuben about this? What does he suggest?'

'He suggested buying a house and then went on about shares and investments, and I got so lost it made no sense to me at all!'

Josh laughs a little, then says, 'Do you mind if I take the page with me so that I can do some sums and come up with a proposal for you?'

'Oh, please do, and thanks so much! I don't want to impose, though. You're so busy as it is.'

'Nonsense, what are friends for anyhow?'

I look at him and smile because I do not know what else to do. It's the first time he has called us friends, and it feels good.

'Let me know if there is any other information you need, and thanks again, I appreciate it.'

Josh leaves and, because the day is almost over, I remain seated on the sofa, pondering the past few hours and how Josh has become a friend to me.

CHAPTER THIRTY-TWO

The informal celebration is a great success. I know that, by this token of appreciation from the De Lucases, they will maintain the happy vibe that Rio Adventures always had.

The new boardroom, finally finished, takes up the entire top floor of the new wing, and the old boardroom is now divided into two offices – one for Josh and the other for me. De Luca is keeping his old office as is, and Josh's old office is now our private lounge and boardroom. I am grateful that the move won't take up too much of my time, as my office already occupies half the boardroom. It will only be a matter of finishing a few touches, installing plug points, and installing a filing cabinet. I learn from De Luca, as he walks past me in the morning, that Josh will be taking over my office and that I am to move into the other one. So, there is a little more moving, packing, and unpacking than I expected, but at least I should be able to do it in a day.

I knock on Josh's door.

'Come in, Tali. You need never knock, please just come in!'

'Your office looks nice,' I say as I look around.

His desk is to the left, so he always has a view to stare at, something he seems to do a lot. There is a long black sofa at the other end, with a glass coffee table in front of it. There are two light blue armchairs in front of his desk and several portraits on the walls.

'Are those family portraits?' I ask as I look at the biggest one hanging above the sofa. 'Yes, the De Luca ancestors. On the left is my father when he was fifteen, and next to him are his parents, and the others are his grandparents,' he replies proudly.

'It's lovely,' I say, and I'm not just kind.

Josh pulls out a small pile of papers, picks up his pen, and moves to the sofa, motioning for me to join him. I have brought my coffee with me and places it on the coffee table.

'Can I get you some coffee?' I ask.

'No thanks, just had a cup.'
Josh gives me his very impressive proposal, explaining and discussing every point with me so that I clearly understand.
'Gosh, I hope this didn't take you very long, you have gone into so much detail, thank you so much.'
'No, not too long, and don't worry, it was my pleasure.'

That evening, we have a perfectly home-cooked meal as only my mum can make, after which I present what Josh had given me to my mum and Eric.
'He has made such an effort for you, Talia-May, it is very kind of him,' my mum remarks, just as impressed as I was.
'I know, and I told him so.'
After making more coffee, I rejoin them at the table, the papers sprawled out as they inspect them.
'Could you ask Minister Wade to come over one evening so we can tell him, Mum?' Eric asks.
'Why don't we ask him and Jackie to come for lunch on Sunday after service?' My mum suggests, and we agree.
'Perhaps you should ask Josh to come too, in case Minister Wade has any questions?' My mum grins, knowing I will object.
'Uh, no, if he has any further questions, he can phone Minister Wade himself,' I reply quickly.
 As much as I enjoy my newfound friendship with Josh, I am still uneasy in the company of other men, other than at the office and church. We eagerly talk about the new bus and the orphanage, how God has blessed us with the ability to fill this great need, and what Minister Wade's reaction will be to Josh's proposal. We also agreed that our donation to any project will remain anonymous. The glory will be as it should be - given to God. Dad and Cole, we are sure, would want it this way.

On my way to work, I stop to buy a local newspaper and excitedly turn straight to the house sales section as soon as I'm at my desk.
'Gosh, there are so many!' I close the newspaper, sigh, and dump it in the recycle bin. *I will have to find a different route to buy a house.*

I notice Josh coming out of the elevator and run to catch him before he reaches his office.

'Morning, Josh,' I say, not waiting for him to reply, 'I showed your proposal to my mum and Eric last night, and they were both very impressed and asked me to thank you. We are meeting with Minister Wade on Sunday to discuss it further.'

'Good morning, Tali, glad I could help. Please call me if your minister has any questions.'

He opens his office door and stands aside to let me walk in first. I do and sit down on one of the light blue chairs.

'Can I get you some coffee?' I ask.

'No, I'm fine thanks, had two cups before I left home.'

'That's normal for me,' I say, turning to him as he hangs his coat on the coat stand.

'I've noticed you like your coffee,' he replies with a smile.

I turn around quickly and think to myself, *He is so observant.*

'So, what does our day look like today?' He asks as he sits down behind his desk.

'Actually, it's a relatively quiet day. The most important thing is to finalize the billboard ad for marketing. The deadline is Friday.'

'Have you seen it?' He asks, and I nod. 'And, what do you think?'

'I like it. It's humorous and very catchy.'

'Yes, I thought so too. Well, good, then I can go to marketing today. Tali, you haven't taken your leave yet?'

'No, not yet, I'm hoping it will get overlooked. Going on leave will mean I'll be alone. You understand, don't you?' I immediately withdraw at the thought of being alone.

'Of course, I understand, Tali, but isn't there anyone that you can take with you?'

'No, not really, all my friends are married except Jackie, but she's afraid of flying, my mum refuses flatly, and Eric's also not interested, so it just leaves me.'

I know I sound sad, but it's not intentional.

'Well, if you ask me, I think you should still go somewhere. Sometimes, different scenery is all you need to make things better.'

I get the impression he is talking from experience, but I don't dare ask.

'Isn't there someplace you've always dreamed of visiting?'

'No, not really. Cole and I always spoke of places, but they would always be places where the surf was good. I don't think I want to go to those places now,' I smile, trying to hide the stab of pain that cuts my heart in half.

'If you consider Italy, I have family all over the country, and I know they would gladly have you as their guest. They love having visitors, and they're the best tour guides in the world.'

'Oh, gosh, thank you, that is very kind of you, but I think for now I just want to go somewhere here in South Africa. Maybe try an adventure holiday with this company called Rio Adventures, I hear they're outstanding.' I giggle.

Josh laughs out loud. I've never heard him laugh like this before, and it's very infectious and makes me want to laugh even more.

'Hmmm, I think you should get hold of them,' he says, laughing some more. 'Honestly, Tali, put in for a month's leave and go somewhere, please! Ask if you need any help, okay.'

I thank him and leave, but don't go back to my office. Instead, I go to Cheri and Sondra.

What will they say about this?

Of course, they think it's a great idea, fancying the Italy idea immensely. Gina did a lot of traveling in her youth and loved Italy, so of course, she promotes the idea with zeal. Even though they're enthusiastic, I'm not remotely excited about the whole idea. I try to convince myself that once I'm away, seeing different faces and different walls, it will be the right thing for me.

That will still take a lot of convincing, I think.

Eventually, when I head back to my office, I have destination options coming out of my ears. I know I can afford to go anywhere I desire, but that's just the problem. I don't want to go anywhere without Cole.

Like Josh's office, my desk is also to the left, facing the right wall, which gives me a view out the window all day. My office is not as big as his, but I also have a sofa against the right wall and a coffee table in front of it. There is a filing cabinet against the wall next to the door and a table with a coffee machine next to it. For the moment, that is all, and for the moment it is good enough.

I read through my emails with a cup of coffee in hand, my mind going back to the issue of my leave as I open an email from the World Tourism Bureau. It's an invitation to a tourism convention to be held in Geneva in two months, at the end of September. Suddenly, I know.
This is it!
Yes, I could go to the convention with the De Lucases and then stay on for a few weeks. This way, I won't feel like I'm traveling completely alone. Now I start to feel a little excited about taking my leave. I know the De Lucases go to this convention every year, so it will not be a matter of convincing them to let me go along.
Yes, this will be the perfect thing for me. I grin and nod my head, pleased.

I print the email and decide to discuss it with the De Lucases in tomorrow's meeting. I will speak to my mum, Eric, and Minister Wade on Sunday to hear their opinions, but for now, I go straight to Cheri, Sondra, and Gina. When I tell them, they agree with gusto and immediately look it up on Google, point out interesting places, print me a list of accommodation options, and what not to miss.

I'm too excited to wait until Sunday, so I call my mum. She is enthusiastic, but not enough to convince her to join me. When I get home, I phone Eric and try to convince him that he and Judith should join me, but that comes to naught as well. I thought I would be more disappointed with their responses, but as I lie on my bed with Cole's photo in my arms, I realize I'm not. Maybe going on my own will be a good thing, but before I make that decision, I'll still ask Garth and Merle if they would join. I fall asleep with my mind running through the places we found on Google, what I could say to Garth and Merle, and what I will say to the De Lucases. I wish, oh how I wish that

Cole could go with me. He would be so excited. I pray that God continues to show me the path I should take, to continue to give me the strength to get through each day, and to help me make sense of it all.

CHAPTER THIRTY-THREE

Mr. De Luca arrives late for the first time since I can remember, and he offers no excuse, only an apology. Mr. De Luca, Josh, and I sit at the boardroom table in our private lounge and discuss a few other business matters and progress reports before the opportunity presents itself to bring up the Geneva Tourism Convention. Naturally, they know about it, having also received the email, and, as I expected, ask me to join. This is when I take the chance to speak to them about my holiday plans.

'Um, Josh, you said I should take my leave soon, well, would it be possible to stay perhaps in Geneva for a while after the convention, if it does not clash with any work-related issues?'

I hold my breath nervously.

Maybe they will not agree to it, and then I will be back to square one with this whole leave matter.

'That, Tali, is a brilliant idea!' Mr. De Luca exclaims.

I was expecting Josh to reply first.

'Really? Oh, thank you! I will make all the arrangements for us and then email you the travel itinerary. I will put in for my leave today and let you know the dates. Do you want me to arrange a temp for the time I am away?' I say excitedly, Josh smiling at me approvingly as if to say, "I told you so."

'No, not to worry about that, we will cope here. If you check your emails every so often and forward any that need our attention to me, we'll be just fine.'

The meeting ends, and I rush off to Cheri to sign the necessary leave forms.

'Tali, this is great, you've never taken leave except for one or two days here and there, this will be so great for you, so, here you go – an approved leave form from the fifteenth September until the thirtieth September.'

She stands and hugs me, Sondra and Gina do too, and happily, I hurry back to my office to phone Garth.

At my desk, I hesitate. Uncertain, I pick up the phone, dial, and wait for Garth to answer. After a long debate, he agrees to consider my offer, and after tonight's young adults' meeting, we will discuss it further with Merle. Garth is not happy about me paying for everything, and I have to use all my wits to convince him that it is Cole's money I will use and that he would want it. Maybe there is a little emotional blackmail on my part, but I anxiously hope it will work on Merle, too.

At the young adults' get-together, we receive an invigorating lesson from one of the members, Anthony, about opportunities that go missing because of a natural fear of rejection, and how perhaps because of our fears, we go through life not knowing Jesus. He goes on to say how we are responsible for planting the seeds, and so what if we get rejected, all we have to do is plant a seed, and God will do the rest.

For a while, I sit and contemplate what was said in the open discussion, and how easy it is to skip the planting, always thinking there will be another opportunity. But will there be? What if that had happened with Cole? It would have been too late now to plant any seeds, and I would have regretted it for the rest of my life. We leave with a new eagerness and a lack of fear to spread the Word.

We drive in convoy to Garth and Merle's. Sitting in their lounge, with a cup of coffee between my hands, I wonder if perhaps a seed got planted here and whether it will sow. 'I told Merle what you offered today,' Garth says, putting his coffee on the table, but before he can finish his sentence, Merle leans over and throws her arms around me. My coffee spills, but she carelessly laughs.
'Of *course,* we are going, oh, Tali! Thank you so much!' She is clearly excited, 'I know Garth has a bit of a problem with you paying for us,' she laughs, 'but I don't!' And she bursts out laughing again.
'Tali, thank you so much, this will be so good for Garth, you know what I mean,' she whispers into my ear as she hugs me again.

'When do you want to go? I can't remember the dates you said the convention is?' Garth asks, still not too excited.

'The convention is from the twelfth of September until the fourteenth of September, and then we can stay on until the thirtieth of September. If you don't want to fly with me, you can always join me on the Monday or whenever it suits you.'

'Okay, I will make the arrangements at work. You will, I take it, do all our flight bookings then?'

Garth is still so calm.

Merle stands and then sits, her mind racing with ideas. She wonders aloud about the things she will have to pack, especially for Cole Jnr.

'Yes, I will make all the bookings, you just let me know when, and then I will need your IDs and passports for the visas.'

'Okay, there is one more thing, though, for me, I'm not sure about Merle,' he stops, looks at Merle, then continues, 'but I want to get baptized before we leave.'

Merle and I fall silent. He smiles, enjoying our surprise.

'Really? Really? Oh goodness, Garth, this is fantastic! Oh, Cole is rejoicing big time right now!' I rush over to hug him, elated.

'Merle, what do you think?' Garth asks her, seemingly a little unsure of her reaction.

'Oh, Garth, I've been waiting so long for you to commit, dear, I'm so happy.' Tears spill down her cheeks as she reaches for her husband, and I say a silent prayer, thanking God for this decision, for the seed Cole planted that has grown in God's radiance.

I know Minister Wade will not mind being disturbed so late with this news, so I phone him. He rejoices as he speaks to Garth and Merle individually and arranges to meet with them after work tomorrow. When I say my prayers before going to sleep, I praise God for the souls who will be added to His Kingdom and ask God to help me help them in their walk with Him.

Garth, Merle, Minister Wade, Jackie, and most of the young adults from our church, along with Bob, Jeny, Eric, Judith, my mum, and me, are all cramped into my mum's little house after church on Sunday. My mum loves every minute of the hustle and bustle, busying herself with the food, even though everyone has brought a dish of some sort. She has cooked up her usual storm – from roasts to salads to our favorite malva pudding.

With the satisfied and rather bloated stomachs we are boasting, we sit outside in the cool winter sun, no one daring to move too quickly for fear of bursting at the seams.

How can there still be so much food left over? Did we not eat it all?

Minister Wade gladly accepts the responsibility of removing it later to give to the shelter, and no one argues, as no one could eat even one more morsel. Much later, when our bodies can move again, we make our way down to our favorite spot on the beach, where we said goodbye to Cole and where Garth loves to surf. Garth, Merle, and Minister Wade stand shivering in the sea, clutching their arms to keep their bodies warm. We watch as the minister speaks softly to them, his words drifting over the ocean. I think back to that cold night just over a year ago when Cole gave his life to God, and my heart warms. How much has happened since then, how God has worked His greatness in so many people's lives by taking two to be with Him. Although I so much wish Cole were here to witness this occasion, I know that from above, he is rejoicing. I hold Cole Jnr as he watches, fascinated by what his parents are doing. He reaches for Merle as she emerges from the sea, her lips blue from the cold. Jackie covers them in towels, and as soon as they aren't dripping anymore, we embrace them, then join hands in a circle and pray for them – for God to guide them and for all of us to be their support as they start their lives anew.

Much later, after everyone has gone home except Minister Wade and Jackie, we tell him we will be buying the bus. We also tell him about our plans for the orphanage and that we wish to remain anonymous. Minister Wade remains silent for a few seconds and then bends his head and clasps his hands together. We presume he is saying a prayer of thanks, but when he looks up, we see his eyes brimming with tears.

'Thank you. God bless you, all of you, thank you.' The tears trickle down his face. They are happy tears as he smiles with joy radiating from him.

'Don't thank us, dear,' my mum replies, 'it is God we must thank, it is all His work, and we are just the instruments.'

Once again, when I finally get to bed, my mind turns over all the different things that have to get done. I try to remember everything. Eric will do the bus deal, Minister Wade will take the next steps with the orphanage in conjunction with the sponsors, and I have to arrange the flights and the holiday to Geneva. Somewhere amongst all these thoughts, I finally drift into a deep sleep.

CHAPTER THIRTY-FOUR

With everything that's been going on over the past few weeks, I've been relatively happy, but not today. Waking up on the anniversary of Cole and my dad's death is a day I wish could pass by unnoticed, but it's upon me like a massive thundercloud, dark, gloomy, and full of violence. I know, oh how I know that this is God's plan, yet deep inside of me, there is a niggling of anger. I wish that all this pain were just a bad dream and that I would wake up with Cole sleeping next to me, his curly blonde hair messily arranged around his beautiful, gentle face.

I want to go back to sleep and let this day pass by without acknowledging it at all. I want to speak to no one and see no one, but it's not going to be this way. The keys to the bus are being handed over to Minister Wade and all the members of the church today. Although it won't be a big occasion, it still means I have to face people. People who are very aware of what day it is today – people who will be sympathetic, hug me, and tell me how sorry they are.

Kind people who care, Tali! I reprimand myself.

Still, it does not encourage me to get out of bed, and I remain under my duvet with Cole's photo clutched to my chest.

It's a far better option to feed my self-pity and sorrow, I think to myself.

My cell phone rings and my mum on the other end says, 'Morning dear, how're you feeling?' She sounds fine and continues to amaze me.

'Hi Mum, not well.'

'It's okay to feel this way, love, it's normal, we are, after all, human.'

I clear my throat and wipe away my tears with the edge of the duvet, and sitting up, I reply, 'Thanks, Mum, how are you, you okay?'

'Oh yes, I'm fine, I'm looking forward to the service today and giving them the keys to the bus, it's fitting that it gets done today.'

Her excitement is unwittingly contagious.

'Yes, I suppose it is the perfect day on which to do it, I'm just not sure my heart feels the same.'

'I'll pick you up, dear, we can drive together or not?'

'Oh, that'll be great, Mum. Thanks, Mum, I love you.'

Minister Wade delivers a very thought-provoking and inspiring sermon that could only have been delivered with the help of the Holy Spirit. I sit motionless, grasping at every word and absorbing it, feeling guilty for being so self-obsessed and for allowing self-pity to be my master. How small I've made Jesus in my life when he suffered for me and gave His life for me. With my new frame of mind, I welcome everyone who, with nothing but kindness in their hearts and a love of Jesus, encourages me on this day that holds such a memory. Minister Wade hands the keys to Uncle Dan, who immediately gets on the bus and starts it, to a loud round of applause. The elderly get in to take the first trip in it to their retirement home. Eric, Judith, Mum, and I stand proud as we suddenly notice a sign on the back of the bus that reads:

In loving memory of Leon Medeck and Cole Mellors, God be with you till we meet again.

Our surprised expressions amuse Minister Wade, who is standing next to us, and he whispers, 'Sorry, I just had to do that, we are so grateful, it's the least we could do, hope you don't mind.'

We all shake our heads. Words are not necessary, and in any case, we are too choked up to say anything. Minister Wade embraces us as the enormity of the moment takes hold of him. I'm sure that most people will put two and two together and figure out who the bus is from, but that's okay, I guess.

CHAPTER THIRTY-FIVE

My seat in first class is spacious and comfortable. *Flying like this could easily become a rather pleasant habit,* I think to myself as I snuggle under the soft blanket provided by the airline.

The De Lucases fly first class all the time, so they take it in their stride, whereas I observe everything that moves and does not move, in utter awe. I am pleased I've booked Garth and Merle in first class as well, and with Cole Jnr, they will be sure to have a more relaxed thirteen-hour flight. Since it's now late evening, most of the passengers are sleeping, reading, or watching something on the small TV screens. I opt to fall asleep to the gentle motion of the plane - the constant hum is a lullaby to my ears.

'Tali, Tali, wake up!' I hear a whisper in my ear and feel a nudging on my arm that forces me to open my eyes. I squint, and the first thing I see is Josh looming over me.
'We land in about an hour; I thought you might want to freshen up a bit before then.'
I look past him to a lovely lady standing behind him, holding a tray of coffee and food that smells delicious.
Oh goodness, what must I look like? I was going to make sure I woke up before they could see me with my morning face!
On a good day, it's enough to make any scary movie scary.
'Oh, thank you, yes, I will, thanks.'
I wait until he goes back to his seat before I have my coffee and a blueberry muffin. Wiping crumbs off my face, I make my way to the bathroom and can't help noticing a slight smile on Josh's face as I walk past him.
Argh, there goes any good impression I've ever made on the De Lucases.

'It's gorgeous,' I keep saying, totally amazed at the quaint buildings, the ancient history that every building oozes, the

ornate doors and window frames, and even the rooftops that seem to be bragging, 'I'm old, and I've lived to tell the tale.'
While I unpack in the cutest hotel room I've ever seen – granted, I haven't seen many – I look out of the window onto Lake Geneva. The view is breathtaking.
It looks like a painting. The water is a deep blue and dead still, not a ripple runs along the surface, not a breeze disturbs its peace, and sun rays sparkle and dance on the surface. A knock on the door interrupts my masterpiece.
'Would you like to join us for breakfast, before we go to the conference center?'
'Thanks, I would love that, this place is so gorgeous!'
Josh lets out a loud guffaw, and I look at him, confused, wondering what he finds so funny.
'I'm sorry,' he says, holding in another laugh, 'it's just that you've said that about a thousand times already and it's so amusing to watch you take everything in.'
'I'm not sure if that's a compliment or an insult. I think we'd better go before I say it again.' I pick up my bag and smile as I close the door behind me.

Mr. and Mrs. De Luca are already sitting at our assigned table, and Josh, his manners always perfect, holds out a chair for me. Mr. De Luca stands up until I am seated and comfortable. I instinctively feel as though I've been flown into a different era in time, almost expecting the men to be wearing suits all day and the women to be in long dresses carrying parasols.

After a scrumptious breakfast, we head for the conference. The De Luca men walk into the conference room in front of Mrs. De Luca and me. They greet people left, right, and center - clearly, after being in this business for so many years, they have made many acquaintances. They introduce me to every person, and by the time I'm in my seat, I don't recall a single name. Mrs. De Luca chats to me continuously, holding onto my arm as we walk along, and it feels so natural. I don't feel lost or as alone as I expected.

Each day follows pretty much the same routine. Representatives from their respective countries promote their homeland. As this is my first time, I am fascinated and enthralled by places I never even knew existed. Mrs. De Luca gives me a running commentary of all the countries and places mentioned, so much so that later I ask Mr. De Luca why we even bother to have this conference every year, Mrs. De Luca can do it all by herself. Everyone is amused and appreciates my little joke.

On the last evening, a formal dinner is hosted at the hotel. The De Lucases collect me on their way down to the dance hall, and as we make our way to our table, they stop, as usual, to speak to almost everyone we pass. I still cannot remember all their names, but I do, however, remember their faces and which country they represent. In the main entrance to the grand hall, I stand slightly behind Josh, not purposely; it is just the way it has panned out. A gentleman smiles at him and says something to him in Italian, which makes him blush.

I cannot help my surprised expression as he turns around, grinning, 'This man thinks we're engaged and wants to wish us a wonderful life together.'

I look at Josh, horrified.

How do I respond to this? I think as the pain pierces my heart.

I look down at the engagement ring Cole so lovingly gave to me, which I dutifully still wear. Josh replies in Italian and sets the record straight. The man picks up my hand, covers it with his other hand, and rambles off something, which I presume is an apology.

When he leaves, I turn to Josh, 'What did he say?'

Josh, still a little embarrassed, explains, 'He offered his deepest apologies and sympathy for your loss, and said he did not mean to insult you in any way and…' He trails off intentionally.

I do not push the matter, as Mr. De Luca insists we make our way to our table like everyone else.

Once we've eaten mouthwatering traditional food from almost every country represented at the conference, including our South African Bobotie, while consuming far too much Swiss wine, we are entertained by dancers and performers in true Genevan tradition. Mrs. De Luca explains the meaning of every performance to me, and Josh adds his two cents' worth now and then. The evening is so enjoyable, as we laugh and talk with each other and our fellow attendees, that all too soon it comes to an end. It has been a very long time, in fact, since the "oldies' evening," that I've had so much fun and enjoyed other people's company so much.

As I stand at the boarding gates watching the De Lucases depart, I thank them for the umpteenth time for such a wonderful few days. I feel a little guilty about staying behind, but then I think of Garth and Merle, who will be arriving within the hour, and the guilt slowly fades as excitement takes over.

On our way to the hotel, Merle cannot get over the buildings' amazing texture and the heritage held within their walls. I grin as I think of Josh commenting on my reaction to Geneva. Our two weeks fly by, and we spend our time together boating on Lake Geneva, visiting historical sites such as the Cathedrale St-Pierre, several fabulous historical and art museums, and the inspiring Red Cross Museum. We take the most breathtaking scenic drives to the tiny neighborhoods and the hotels and restaurants at the base of the Alps. We admire how the Alps stand and wait silently and patiently for the winter and the influx of tourists that will invade their slopes for the holidays. Geneva is much smaller than any of us imagined, and it fills us with admiration and respect. Garth, Merle, Cole Jnr, and I love every minute of our trip, as we stroll along the cobbled streets, enjoying the warm sunshine, not half as hot as South Africa's scorching sun. Even the language barrier we encounter in most of the shops and restaurants does not dampen the affection we feel for this beautiful country.

Saying goodbye, as we board the plane, we have mixed feelings – on the one hand, we want to stay in this peaceful, beautiful country, but on the other hand, we can't wait to go home. Cole Jnr sleeps in my arms as we take off and head for home. The holiday with Garth, Merle, and Cole Jnr was amazing and just what I needed to rejuvenate myself and get on with my life.

As Garth said one day while we watched a perfect sunset, 'Cole will always be with us in our souls and our hearts, but dwelling on his loss does not help us move forward.'

Since he understood God's plan of salvation, the meaning of life, and what a great and mighty God we serve, he has been able to let go of his heartache. He has been looking forward to the day when he and Cole will meet again. I contemplate his words as I look out of the window onto mounds of clouds, and realize how true they are and that it is time for me to embrace them.

CHAPTER THIRTY-SIX

I knock on Mr. De Luca's door.

'Come in,' comes the reply as it always does.

Since I've been back from Geneva, if it weren't for the photos and the memories imprinted in my mind, I would not have known I'd been away. The daily routine goes on as usual.

'Tali, good morning, please sit,' Josh motions for me to take a seat in one of the chairs in front of Mr. De Luca's desk.

Immediately, I wonder what I've done wrong and begin to get nervous, fidgeting with my hands as I sit down.

'Tali, it's almost December. What are we going to do for our year-end function?'

I breathe a sigh of relief, think about it for a while, and then say, 'Please don't be offended, but, um, if I go by what I've heard most people say about these functions, uh.' I take another breath, 'they would rather you use the money for bonuses and perhaps have something small and simple here at the office.'

I let out a breath and wait nervously, not sure what their reaction will be.

Have I gone too far, been too outspoken?

My hands start to fidget again.

They are silent for a few seconds, then converse in Italian. I am used to this procedure by now, so I wait nervously and patiently, unseeingly staring out of the window.

Finally, Josh says, 'You see, this is why we knew this position would suit you so well! It's an excellent and logical suggestion. Thank you, Tali, for being so honest with us. If you let me know by Friday, when and how much having a function here will cost, we will work out the bonuses accordingly.'

Now I think is a good time to approach them about the Christmas party for the orphanage. I promised Minister Wade I would ask them when the occasion presents itself.

'If I might ask you both something, I know it is on a personal level, but it could benefit the company as well,' I wait, holding my breath, for affirmation before I continue. Josh nods. 'The church has an orphanage up and running, and there are already a few children living there. And for Christmas, we want to give them gifts, have Father Christmas, put up decorations, and have a little party. To make them feel the Christmas spirit, you know. It helps with the bonding, um, in any case, I wonder if it will be possible for Rio Adventures to give a donation of some sort.'

I stop talking, wondering whether what I said came out correctly and whether it made any sense at all. Suddenly, I remember the other half of my speech I prepared.

'Oh yes, sorry, I just remembered! If you want, it can be used as publicity for both the orphanage and for Rio Adventures.'

I stop talking again.

Maybe I should make a run for the door now before they kick me out?

I wait and start fidgeting once more.

They chat in Italian for quite a long period, which makes me even more nervous as I sit dead still in my chair, looking at the floor, not daring to look at their faces. As Mr. De Luca begins to speak, I look up nervously.

'Tali, you certainly have brought a bag of surprises along with you this morning. If you put together a proposal outlining what we can contribute, when, and how we can get involved, we will certainly look at it very seriously. We think this is a wonderful opportunity publicity-wise for us – not that we want to take away anything from the reason behind it – but as you said, the publicity could work both ways.'

He stops talking, but I am still listening.

I did it; I slowly think to myself.

'Thank you so much. I'm sorry if I have gone beyond my boundaries, I, uh, thank you,' I mumble, not knowing what else to say. I get up and make my way to the door, and as always, Josh walks with me and opens the door for me.

'I'd like to work with you on this project if you would allow me,' he says, his eyes twinkling.

'Gladly, that will be much appreciated, Josh, thank you very much.'

I reach my office and dive for the phone to call Minister Wade. As I repeat the conversation with the De Lucases, he becomes filled with gratitude and makes me transfer the call to Mr. De Luca to thank him personally. Then I phone my mum and Eric to tell them the news, and rush to Cheri, Sondra, and Gina for coffee and croissants.

Back in my office, I immediately begin working on the year-end function costs, excitedly thinking about the orphanage. A Skype message pops up on my screen:

My father has told my mother about your orphanage project, and she apparently got very excited about it. She has asked to help in any way she can; this is a very good thing you're doing here, Tali.

I stare at the screen.

What should I say? I ponder.

Your mum is welcome to help. This will be wonderful. Please don't give me any credit; this is Minister Wade's project, and I am merely the messenger. I am just so grateful that you and your father are willing to listen.

Not long after our Skype conversation, my phone rings, and another Skype message from Josh appears on my screen at the same time. I answer the phone first. It is Minister Wade.

'Hello Tali, gosh, those bosses of yours sure do move fast. Josh just phoned me now to request that you and I attend a meeting with them, whenever it suits you.' The excitement in his voice is touching.

'I'm busy reading a Skype message from him now about it. So I guess I no longer have to worry about a proposal like he originally requested. This is wonderful! Honestly, any time is fine with me. I am here all the time, let me know when it will suit you, and we can take it from there.'

'Okay, I'll phone you back in a few minutes.'

I finish up the year-end staff function costs, pleased that it works out to such a minimal amount, and email them to Josh. Happy with the turn of today's events, I switch off my computer, collect my belongings, and make my way to my mum's.

CHAPTER THIRTY-SEVEN

Two days to go to the orphanage's Christmas party. The planning has gone swiftly and without any hiccups, and the little children still have no idea about it – complete surprise is what we are aiming for and have achieved so far. Mrs. De Luca and my mum have been incredible, coming together with the same ideas in mind. My mum introduced Mrs. De Luca to her girlfriends, and since then, it's as though they've always been friends. They did all the shopping together, and they've had an absolute blast. Mr. De Luca and Josh call them 'old ladies on a mission,' which brings on a roll of laughter every time.

Our final meeting with the local newspaper and photographers will be held later today. The staff from Rio Adventures and GB Tours will also join the meeting, as they will be at the party as well. It has grown into a combined Christmas party for the children at the orphanage, the staff's children, and the children from the church. Minister Wade's rationale for all the planning is that the orphanage children can mix with other children and gain friends and confidence in the process. I admire the way his mind works, always for the good of making even just one person's life better.

My mum and I are the first to arrive at the orphanage, aside from Minister Wade and Jackie. The little children are buzzing around us and seem to sense that something exciting is about to happen today. We start carrying in boxes of decorations, snacks, drinks, and party accessories from the car, and all the little hands are eager to help. The kids' smiles and curious eyes warm my heart so much, and I know I'll be in tears of joy by the end of the day.

Minister Wade instructs all of us to carry the boxes to the dining hall or the 'mess hall' as he calls it, referring to what it looks like after dinner. Two huge wooden doors lead from the dining hall to an enclosed garden with jungle gyms, a trampoline, and a few benches, kindly donated by some church members, where we will be having the party. Slowly, people who had promised to help are starting to arrive. With a jovial atmosphere, lots of laughs, and playing around, we eventually manage to make the outside area look like a party, much to the delight and explosive excitement of the children.

At times, I am not too sure who is enjoying this more, the children or the adults, in particular, Mr. De Luca, who spends more time playing with the children than helping us set up. He runs after them with hats on his head, making them squeal with laughter, and at times, tears roll down our faces from laughing so hard.

'I apologize for my father's antics. I guess my being an only child and not having provided him with any grandchildren yet has deprived him somewhat,' Josh grins at me as we stand together enjoying the entertainment.

'Is he always like this around children?' I ask, wiping the tears from my face.

'Oh yes, he loves children! He always says he regrets not having had more, and is forever complaining that I have not given him any grandchildren yet.'

'I would never have thought this of your father! No insult intended, it's just that he's so refined and professional at work, I suppose it's the only side we get to see at the office.'

'None taken. Yes, he is very different from the office.' Josh replies as a little girl comes screeching up to me, grabs my legs to hide behind, and almost knocks me over. Josh seizes my arm to stop me from falling over. I pick her up, and we run to hide behind the jungle gym as she giggles, screeches, and laughs from the depths of her stomach. It's such a contagious laugh that paralyzes me. I laugh so much I cannot move, and I collapse onto the lawn, hanging on to her tightly. She throws her arms around me as we lie on the grass. Giggling, she swings her head from side to side to see where Mr. De Luca is and who he's busy chasing after now. Eventually, thank goodness, Mr. De Luca runs out of steam, and we can all get finished and get our breath back. The children are so worked up by now that they continue jumping on the trampoline and running around just for the sake of it. As parents from the office and church start to arrive, their children join in the fun. It is a mass of kids running up and down, laughing, screeching, talking rapidly, falling, getting up, and doing it all over again. It is fantastic.

Garth and Merle arrive with Cole Jnr, whom I immediately relieve from his mom. I take him for a walk among the playing children. His fascination with the chaos that resonates is expressed in the delighted look on his little face. The girl I was tumbling on the lawn with is four-year-old Coco, who introduces herself merrily to Cole Jnr. Her mop of long black hair, her piercing green eyes, and her olive complexion make her a beautiful little girl, and she kindly attaches herself to me. I find out from Minister Wade that her parents – her father, a Greek, and her mother, Spanish – lived in South Africa for many years. They were killed in a boating accident when Coco was two, and she has been in foster care ever since.

'HO HO HO,' a deep voice sounds from the dining hall. All the children freeze on the spot for a second or two, then look toward the sound.
'HO HO HO,' the voice sounds again, and then, to the delight of the children, Santa emerges from the wooden doors. Some kids become a little afraid of this strange-looking man with such a loud voice, but soon get caught up in the festive spirit and follow the rest of the children as they clamor around Santa. Mr. De Luca kneels and asks the children who on earth this strange man is and what he could have in his big red bag.
'Maybe, just maybe, if you all give Santa a huge, big group hug, he will show you what's in the bag?' Mr. De Luca suggests.
They jump up and down and tug on Santa's suit.
'Poor Santa,' I mutter, and we all laugh. 'Is that Greg?' I ask, 'I can't believe he had to do it!'
All the men at work had to draw straws to be Santa because none of them were exactly willing. The lot, to his horror, fell on Greg. However much he complained, he is doing brilliantly, picking up some of the children, a few at a time, too. He

hobbles over to the Christmas tree, a string of children and Mr. De Luca in tow. He sits down on his chair and speaks to the children for a while.

'Have you been good? Do you know who I am? Do you know what is in the big red bag?'

Each time the kids answer in a loud combined shout, followed by laughter. I look around at the adults circling the children, all of them watching, smiling, and laughing with as much delight as the children, and my mum and Mrs. De Luca are clapping each time the kids answer correctly.

I think to myself, *How perfect is this?*

'Why are you thinking so hard?' A voice next to me startles me.

'Oh, Josh, shoo, you frightened me! I'm just looking at everyone's expressions, and see all the happy faces. It's so beautiful.' I smile.

'Yes, it is, it's a good day,' he replies and remains standing next to me.

'HO HO HO,' shouts Santa again.

'HO HO HO,' all the children yell back every time Santa reaches into his big red bag to take presents out.

I only wish I could capture the excited, sparkling wide eyes of each child and store them in a memory box to keep forever.

'Oh, they are just too precious,' is what every second person exclaims as we watch the children rip off the wrapping paper to reveal what Santa brought them.

June keeps the video camera rolling.

'I will get a copy of this, such a blessed day,' I softly say as I feel a thud against my knees.

It's Coco again. She is dancing and jumping up and down, her face lit up like a thousand stars as she shows me a pink box that holds a Barbie doll with an extra set of clothes.

'Open for me, please?' She says over and over.

I take the box from her and sit on the ground next to her so she can watch what I'm doing. Her eagerness overtakes her patience, and she helps me open the box. Once the doll is free from the plastic, she hugs it to her chest, her body swaying from side to side as she tucks her head into her chest to shield her new doll from the world.

Josh kneels next to us, 'What a beautiful doll, sweetie,' he says to Coco, 'is she your friend? What's her name?' His voice is soft, gentle, and comforting.

Coco looks at him, unsure, afraid that if she lets go, her doll might get taken away from her, then she looks to me for reassurance.

'She's beautiful, so she must have a beautiful name,' I say encouragingly to her.

'Princess,' Coco replies softly, slowly taking the doll out of her hold to look at her.

'Yes,' I say, 'that is because she is a princess, isn't she, only a princess is so beautiful.'

She looks at me and then at her doll again, approving of what I've just said. While she sits next to me, she takes out Princess's clothes one by one, rests Princess in her lap, and holds the clothes up against the doll, scrunching up her face in concentration. Merle carries Cole Jnr over, with his toy truck, which he delightedly bangs on her head. She sits him down next to Coco, who shows him her doll and all the clothes. Cole Jnr listens as if he understands, banging his truck on the ground as though in agreement.

I start to stand up from my seated position on the ground, and Josh, ever the gentleman, offers me his hand. Sondra, Cheri, and Gina join us. All the men willingly disappear to get us something to drink.

'Josh seems to have attached himself to you?' Merle says more by asking than by implying.

'Yes, maybe, it's because we've become friends ever since I started working so closely with him, and he doesn't really know anyone else here. He probably feels a bit out of place. I doubt very much that this is his sort of thing.'

'Well, his father is very much at home,' Cheri laughs as she points to De Luca, still encouraging the children to give Santa a hard time.

'Oh my gosh, I know, who would've thought this of Mr. De Luca, he is so funny!'

Coco spends the rest of the afternoon as close to me as possible. I can feel a bond growing between us, and I think that one has developed, as small as it might be, between her and Cole Jnr too. When I say goodbye to her, I hold her hand and promise to come back to visit her every week and to see her every Sunday at church, too. I know we are going to be very good friends for a long time to come.

The local newspaper puts an article about the Christmas party on its front page. A lovely photo of Santa walking out into the garden with his big red bag, while the little children clap their hands and jump up and down, complements a touching article about the day. Minister Wade and Mr. De Luca are going to be delighted, I think, as I sip my coffee and read on.

A tapping on my office door makes me look up. It's Josh, leaning in through the door frame, holding the newspaper in his right hand.
He waves it as he says, 'Great piece, don't you think?'
'It is,' I reply, 'I love the photo. Thank you for everything you and your parents did. It was such a special day.'
'It was indeed,' he answers, waving his paper goodbye at me.
I look closely at the photo again and notice Coco standing at the back, clapping her hands with the rest of the children. I jump up, make twenty copies, pick up the phone, and dial Suzie's number.
'Hi Suzie, it's Tali speaking, can I come to see you quickly?'
I take the twenty copies with me and ask if she will kindly laminate them for me. I explain that I want to give each child at the orphanage a copy so they can remember Santa and their big day.

On my way home from work, I stop at the orphanage. The children are in the playroom, most of them playing with the toy they got from Santa on Saturday. I find Minister Wade helping a little boy build his Lego. I walk in quietly, not wanting to disturb them. Minister Wade gets up to greet me, and I give him the laminated copies of the newspaper article. He hands them out as one by one the kids giggle at themselves in the photo and at, of course, big Santa. Coco sidles up to me, clutching her doll, eager to show off its new outfit and a new hairstyle. She makes herself comfortable on my lap while I chat to Minister Wade.

'Would it be okay if I come around, say, two nights a week and read stories to the children and help tuck them into bed?' I ask.

'Would I mind? Goodness, Tali, definitely not. In fact, I want to ask the members if any of them are willing to do exactly that, at least one night a week. It would mean so much to the children.'

'My dad and Cole would've loved Saturday's party.'

'I know Tali; I could just see them there, laughing their heads off with the rest of us, I know they were watching it all from Heaven, Tali.'

My days are so busy that I barely have time for myself. Every day after work, I go to the young adults' meeting, the youth meeting, the cell group, the orphanage, or my mum's house. Of course, on Sundays, I go to church and afterward to my mum's or Garth and Merle's. This routine suits me immensely as it gives me precious little time to dwell on Cole's absence. Although I will never forget him or stop missing him, the hole that tore my heart apart has slowly begun to heal. Of course, I have moments when it seems like I've not moved on at all, but those moments have become fewer.

Before I know it, it's the third anniversary of my dad and Cole's death. On this emotional day, I spend some time on the beach with Garth and Merle, as we have every year. Cole Jnr has become a strong overgrown toddler with far too much energy. Watching him on the beach, we all agree that one day he will be the tallest, biggest, and most handsome professional surfer ever.

'Are you going to ask anyone to the charity dinner you said Cheri invited you to?' Merle asks, while we watch Cole Jnr building sandcastles and then taking more pleasure in kicking them down and spraying the sand over us.

'Oh, I doubt it,' I reply without hesitation.

'But why not?'

'I've just never thought about it, and I don't see why I have to take someone with me. In any case, I don't know of anyone I could ask.'

'Not true, you can ask Josh.'

'You're kidding, right? Why do you think I should ask my boss? Are you crazy? In any case, I doubt he'd go with me,' I say, surprised and somewhat defensive.

'Well, I think you're wrong. I think he would be very obliging.' Merle is trying hard to convince me.

'Nope, that is not going to happen.'

I want the subject to close, but it isn't, and it bothers me that she would even suggest I ask him.

'Why did you suggest Josh?' I ask, my curiosity eventually getting the better of me.

'I think he's a nice person, Tali. I know he is your boss, but I think you get on so well outside of work too,' Merle slowly replies as though choosing her words carefully.

'Hmm, well, I'm not going to ask anyone, thanks all the same,' I say, not quite as convincing as I would have liked to sound.

Gina chatters away nonstop when I join them for lunch in their office. She is just in one of those moods, but no one minds. We listen and comment whenever we manage to get a word in, and, as always, lunch with Cheri, Sondra, and Gina is pleasant. It is a busy time for all of us at work right now, as we are promoting Rio Adventures and GB Tours to tour companies in Japan, China, and Thailand. The representatives from each country will arrive next week and, as always, last-minute arrangements, schedule changes, and the nitty-gritty of accommodation and transport add extra pressure to what seems to be a well-planned event. One of the reasons I enjoy my lunches with the ladies from the third floor so much is that we all manage, for just an hour most days, to escape the pressures of work. The hour is always up before we know it, and while she walks me to the lift, Cheri asks, 'What are you wearing to the charity dinner?'

'Oh no, what with being so busy at work, I completely forgot about an outfit, and I've only got tomorrow and Friday to figure something out, but I can't get anywhere as it's going to be too hectic.'

Number Two, I think to myself in a Scottish accent, and then, as the doors open, I say to Cheri, 'I'll find something in my cupboard, I'm sure, but if not, you won't mind if I raid yours again, will you?'

I think as I step into the elevator, *"Well done, Number Two."*

I notice Josh leaning against the elevator wall, studying a pile of papers in his hands.

'Of course, you can just let me know,' Cheri says, and turns to go back to her desk as the elevator doors close.

Josh smiles at me as I turn to face the cartooned doors, and he continues to flip through his notes in his folder.

'The beauty of being a woman,' he says in a teasing tone, 'is if you can't buy it, borrow it, and men will never know the difference!'

He chuckles loudly and carries on going through his notes as though he didn't say anything. I feel my cheeks beginning to match the red jersey I'm wearing.

'It's for a charity dinner, Cheri's husband Tian is forcing me to go to on Saturday, and I haven't even given a thought as to what I'm going to wear. I know you men can't grasp the concept that women have to plan this sort of thing, but we do, and I haven't,' I reply teasingly.

He shuts his folder as the elevator doors open, and we both step out, and he walks along next to me in silence.

I turn to go into my office, and before I realize, my mouth is even open, I speak out of turn, 'Would you like to come with me to the charity dinner?'

I stand frozen and shocked, and now I know that my face is as red as my jersey.

Oh, you silly, stupid, stupid woman, are you crazy? I reprimand myself silently, wishing I could swallow my words and never allow them to be repeated.

'Uh, sorry, that was very blunt of me, I'm sure you have far better things to do with your life,' I quickly try to regain my composure.

'Actually,' Josh says with a big smile, 'I would love that. Besides, I don't have anything better to do this weekend. What time should I pick you up?'

'Oh, um, really, are you sure?'

I know it's silly to ask. If there's one thing I've learned about the De Lucases since I've started working so closely with them, it's that they never say anything they do not mean. One of the main reasons I feel so safe with them.

'Of course, Tali, what time would you like me to pick you up?'

'Thank you,' I can still feel how flushed my face is, 'six is fine, I can always meet you at the venue if that's easier?'

'Absolutely not! I will pick you up at six on Saturday, then,' he says defiantly and strides towards his office.

I rush to my desk, open Skype, and send a group message to Cheri, Sondra, and Gina:

I can't believe what I just did. The words were out before I even knew what I was saying. I asked Josh to go to the charity dinner with me, and he said yes...what is wrong with me...? I'm so stupid!!

A barrage of laughs comes back via Skype, and I can see them laughing at me and having the greatest time making fun of my momentary impulsiveness.

What were you thinking, Tali? I ask myself over and over again as I pick up the phone and dial Merle's number.

She gives me the same reaction.

I am not happy with my support group right now, I say to myself.

Well, you've only got yourself to blame for this one, I reply to myself.

For the rest of the day, concentrating seems impossible, and when I get to the young adults' group after work, I get pretty much the same reaction from everyone.

What have I gone and done? Well, it will just be this one time, and I will be sure not to make the same mistake again, that is for sure. I try to convince myself as I battle to fall asleep.

I feel like I'm betraying Cole, but I know that's not true. I'm just annoyed at getting myself into this situation.

I'm grateful that the next two days will be jam-packed, but not at all happy that they will be spent almost entirely with the De Lucases. I park my car in my usual parking space, slowly collect my bag and laptop, and make my way into the building. It is bitterly cold today, and rain is imminent.

'Good morning, Booker,' I say, as he opens the door for me, 'I bet you love this weather, hey?'

'Oh yes, Miss Medeck, I can feel the rain coming,' he replies, as upbeat as always.

'I'm so glad that I'm going to be stuck in the building all day today and tomorrow. It is way too cold for me outside!'

The banter over our difference of opinion on the weather has never ceased since I arrived at Rio Adventures.

I am snug and warm in my office, busily working on schedules and correspondence from airlines and hotels, gulping my coffee before the meeting with the De Lucases. I guess Josh has told his father about my conversation with him, as I'm sure I detect a glint in Mr. De Luca's eyes when I greet him in the boardroom. Josh doesn't seem bothered, and it is business as usual. However, his nonchalant attitude does not ease my immediate agitation, and for the first half an hour or so, I am distracted until I get so wrapped up in the needs in front of me that the feeling leaves me completely.

Finally, after a very long afternoon of meetings with marketing and tour guides, I go to Cheri's house to look for a dress, and then make my way to the orphanage, knowing that Coco will love to see the dress. I wish I could just go to bed and sleep.
'It is so pretty,' Coco keeps saying, her eyes sparkling as she beams and touches the material, 'you're going to look so pretty.'
She holds up the long-sleeved black dress with a round neck in front and a square back. The dress tapers tightly into the waist, then flares into a full skirt to the floor. A small pale green scarf is a great contrast and finishes off the dress with fine elegance.
You can always rely on Cheri's wardrobe; I think smiling.
I enjoy the delight of Coco and all the other little girls as I sway from side to side, holding the dress against me and the skirt out wide so that it swishes and flows with each movement.
'Tali a princesth,' Mika, the youngest of the girls, says. It is too cute.
I pick her up and hug her, 'Thank you, darling.'
All too soon, Nurse Sally comes to take them to their beds. My stay tonight is short-lived because I arrived later than usual. I walk with them, as I always do, holding as many little hands as possible. I make sure they brush their teeth, wash their adorable little faces, and we say a prayer together. Without fail, whenever I leave, my heart nudges a buried sadness, and I feel assaulted with a pang of guilt that I have a home to go to, and they do not. I desperately want to take them all home with me

and make them my family, yet all I can do is blow them goodnight kisses.

'How are you doing?' I ask Nurse Sally as we walk to the kitchen for our usual cup of Milo.
Nurse Sally, experienced beyond her years in child care, is sixty-five years old. Her grey hair is always tied back in a hard ponytail, but it does not take away the softness of her sweet, gentle nature. The children love her and, for her age, she is surprisingly fit.
'I am very well, thanks for asking, it has been a long time since I have loved my work as much as I do here.' The honesty in her voice rings out loudly.
'Well, I cannot imagine anyone else taking such good care of these little darlings.'

With Josh's help and advice, I have the privilege of donating to the orphanage's funding for the next 20 years. I gave up on the idea of buying a house for now because I think contributing to the orphanage is far more important. My mum's house is anyhow free of any debt, and she has grown accustomed to her single life, coming and going as she pleases. So the need for a house with a flat for her is no longer an immediate concern for Eric or me.

CHAPTER THIRTY-NINE

I rush up from the marketing floor with an armful of literature and brochures, all translated into the relevant languages. Spending far too much time with the marketing staff, laughing at ourselves read the brochures aloud. I dump everything on the boardroom table with a thud and make my way to my desk to check my emails before rushing off to another meeting with the hotel where our guests will be staying. A bling from my computer frightens me.

It's a Skype message from Josh:

What colors are you wearing to the charity dinner? I would hate to clash with you.

I laugh out loud, *Oh goodness, since when do men worry about color-coding?*

I vaguely remember trying to color-code with Cole a few times.

I reply:

Black and a very pale green. Please don't go to any great effort.

He replies instantly:

Okay, thanks.

I am in my car and have almost driven off the premises when I realize I've forgotten to bring the brochures and literature. Now I have to hurry all the way back up to the boardroom and then back to my car and jog past Booker each time, much to his amusement. Gratefully, traffic is kind to me, and I make it to the meeting with two minutes to spare. I am so glad it's Friday. Most Fridays, we leave the office earlier than usual, but today there's still just too much to do before our guests arrive on Monday. Our meeting with the hotel company seems to carry on forever and finally finishes at almost 18:00. Mr. De Luca, being the perfectionist that he is wherever his company is concerned, relentlessly focuses on every detail, but by the end of it all, everyone is on the same page and wants the same result. I say yes to a quick cup of coffee, as I pack away my laptop.

Josh sits in the chair next to me and swivels to look at me and says calmly, 'Still six tomorrow then?'

'Yes, please don't bother about the color-coding thing, though, Josh.' I am almost pleading.

'Too late,' he stands up and joins his father as Mr. De Luca walks past.

They bid me goodbye and wish me a good weekend.

'Great. Now people will think we are the color-coding type couple,' I grumble to my cup of coffee.

A knock on the door sounds, and my heart skips a beat as I nervously go to open the door.

'Hello Josh, please come in,' I say as I step back to allow him in.

'Thanks, Tali, you look lovely.' He looks admiringly at me, and I feel my face flush.

He stands in the lounge area, inspecting all my photos. It looks like he's trying to figure out if this is what he imagined my home to be like.

'Thank you, so do you,' and I mean every word.

But then again, Josh always looks smart regardless of what he is wearing. Tonight, he is dressed in a black suit with a white shirt and a pale green tie, and with his dark hair, he looks very handsome indeed. Still nervous, I pick up my bag, put on my coat, and motion for us to leave.

Josh converses casually in the car about daily things and the guests arriving on Monday. I sense he knows I am nervous. I am a little less uncomfortable by the time we arrive at the venue. The décor in the Serenity Hall of the Carmine Hotel is so grand that even in Cheri's exquisite and overpriced dress, I feel out of place.

'Oh goodness, I don't fit in places like this, it's so fancy,' I whisper to Josh.

He chuckles, 'You really have an issue with fancy, don't you?'

He takes my arm as we make our way past the usher, and once we have reached our table, he pulls out my chair to allow me to sit before making himself comfortable.

We chatter idly about the décor and the organization hosting the event while we wait for the others to arrive. Not that I have any information to give Josh regarding this. I'm only here as a favor to Cheri.

'Have you always been a Christian?' Josh asks me out of the blue.

A little surprised, it takes me a few seconds to react without showing my surprise at his question.

'Ever since I can remember! You knew my father, so you know that he lived for God and His church. When I left school, though, I fell away, not my belief or faith, but my commitment. Then, when Cole started asking questions, I realized how far I had slipped away, so as Cole studied more and more and finally was baptized, I found my way back with him,' I reply, more long-winded than I intended.

'Do you ever ask questions, I mean, do you ever blame God or get angry with Him for what happened?' He asks me hesitantly.

I take a deep breath. I have not faced this line of questioning in a long time. The wounds in my heart open so easily, even though it has been a few years already. I take a while before answering, Josh waiting patiently, sipping on his red wine.

'Um,' I clear my throat and shift in my chair, as though this will help me answer him, 'it was tough at first. I tried to explain it to myself over and over again, tried to figure out why God would allow this to happen. Why did it have to happen to my father and Cole? Especially since Cole had just started in his new life as a Christian, you know.'

Again, I shift in my seat, take a sip of my wine, and clear my throat once more. 'I couldn't understand how my mother could be so cheerful, and I couldn't. I always knew I should have been more like her. Then, one day, Minister Wade came to visit me, and we spoke for hours. I knew I couldn't blame God, and all I had to do was accept His greater plan. Questioning Him and trying to find the answers myself would never allow me to move on with my life, and it's not what God teaches.'

I have another sip of my wine, not sure how much I am boring him or whether I am even making any sense.

'There are not many people in this world who would react any differently to the way you did. In fact, most would never recover from it.'

'I have a great support system – my family, the church, and a few very close friends, without them, who knows how I would've got through it,' I reply and pick up my napkin, fiddling with it unconsciously.

'And don't forget your work and colleagues,' Josh says, with a smirk on his face.

I smile, 'Of course, my work and colleagues were an immense help through it all.'

'Sorry, we're late!' Cheri says, interrupting our conversation as she, Tian, Sondra, Neville, Gina, and her husband Jurie take their seats at the table. After feasting on a buffet fit for a king, an auction is held. All the men at our table buy wine at a price far above its value, and Josh also buys a vase, which he says is a gift for his mother. We all dreamily sigh aloud, which makes him blush, and we laugh.

The dance floor is opened by the chairman of the charity organization and his wife, and soon everyone is enjoying themselves, dancing or chatting.

Josh and I join the dancing crowd, and I am comfortable dancing with him like I did that first time at Sondra's wedding. Laughing, we make turn after turn, my dress swishing just as Coco said it would. After several strenuous dances, we are in desperate need of refreshments and make our way back to our table, electing to have grape juice rather than another glass of red wine, afraid we might drink it too fast, being so thirsty.

'You mentioned that Cole got baptized – do you mean a full immersion?' Josh asks, returning to our previous conversation.

'Yes, your body must be completely immersed in the water before you come up again.'

His curiosity about my Christianity forces me to ask him about his.

'Do you believe in God?'

'Well, this might surprise you, but I got baptized when I was twenty-five and still living in Italy,' he says with a smile on his face.

I am sure my bottom lip must be hanging on the floor, so I take a breath to pick it up again, 'Really?'

'I was not always a very nice person, Tali,' he says softly, as though confessing, 'after I got my BCom degree, I went on a gap year to Italy. There, I got involved with the wrong side of my family. I mean the bad people in my family, the drug dealers, and alcoholics. Let's just say, the gutter was a five-star hotel. My aunt, Sophia, hauled me off the street one day and took me straight to her church. It got me thinking about my life and where I had landed up. Grateful as I was to her, I still felt very lost and just couldn't fit in at her church. So, I started looking for a place where I felt comfortable, and I did – after a lot of studying and soul-searching, I got baptized. My aunt was happy for me but not impressed that I hadn't adhered to her beliefs, and she told my father before I could. The next minute, my dad was in Italy and offering me a position at the company. As things were at the time, I didn't have anything else to do, so I left Italy with him, and here I am.'

He raises his hands as he finishes and then lets them rest in his lap again. He looks relieved.

'Why did you never say anything to me?' I reply, picturing this immaculately dressed man lying in a gutter.

'I was afraid of stepping over the employee-employer boundary, I guess.'

'So, where do you worship now?'

'Nowhere at the moment. When I came back, I went to a few churches, but never felt they were right for me. They seemed to be all about money and not the truth, so I haven't been to a worship service in years. I suppose you've noticed me gazing out the window a lot; I am speaking to God. I'm asking Him to give me the right words to say, to treat the people that I will be addressing in a way pleasing to Him. Since I'm not in any church, it's a way for me to stay close to God so that I don't fall away because I'm not with other Christians.'

He stands up and holds out his hand, 'The music is being wasted,' he smiles as he motions to the dance floor.

CHAPTER FORTY

My mum stares at me, her eyes welling with tears. 'You look so beautiful, Talia-May. I'm going to go now before I cry my face into a mess. I love you, my dear.'
She kisses my cheek, hugs me, and leaves. She looks so pretty in her dark green dress – it brings out the sparkle in her eyes, and her hair is all styled up, allowing her face to radiate the happiness inside her.
'Thanks, Mum, I love you so much. See you in a bit!' I say as I fight back my tears.

Maneuvering off the small cushioned stool I've been sitting on, I kneel in front of it, rest my elbows on the cushion, and bring my hands together. I bow my head and close my eyes. As I start to pray, I feel a movement next to me, and, opening my eyes, I see Coco doing the same. I take hold of her little hand and say a prayer aloud.
'Dear Lord, thank you that I am so blessed. I pray, Lord, that you will use me as an instrument for your works. Thank you, Lord, that you have given me a new direction in this life, and, in this new life, I pray that You will be the center point, my pillar, and my rock. Please, Lord, guide me and let your Holy Spirit dwell in me always to do good works for You. In Jesus' name, amen.'
'Amen.' Coco repeats after me.
Coco's face is a picture, no, it's a portrait. Her hair, done up in big curls, is decorated with tiny cream flowers that bounce with every step she takes in her cream princess-style dress.
'We going to start now, Mummy? Is it time? Can I go now?' She asks, without taking a breath after each question, her excitement almost at a level of hysteria.
My heart almost bursts through my ribcage every time I hear her call me 'mummy.' Coco started calling me 'mummy' from the moment we first discussed adoption. I hold out my hands to take hers in mine.

How God has blessed me with this beautiful child! I think to myself, smiling at her.

'Yes, I think it's time, sweetheart.' I say as I hug her carefully, so as not to wrinkle our dresses.

'Yippee,' she squeals and hugs me tightly, releasing me with a kiss, 'I love you, Mummy, you look just like a queen.'

She stares into my eyes, her nose touching mine, her hands holding my cheeks in their tiny palms. Then she giggles and wriggles her way out of our embrace, grabbing her basket and making her way to the door, impatiently waiting for me to join her.

I stand for a few seconds in front of the mirror, a last-minute check of my hair and makeup. I stare at the earrings that Cole gave me almost five and a half years ago, peeking out from beneath my curls. My heart thumps loudly in my chest. They match my hair perfectly, as it falls naturally down my back, the same little flowers as Coco's, sporadically placed in my hair.

'Keep it together,' I mutter aloud to myself.

A slight knock on the door makes Coco jump up and down.

'It's time, it's time, yay!' She opens the door, 'Hello Uncle Eric, look at me, I look so pretty, I'm a princess!' She exclaims as she spins around, making her dress swirl.

'You are the most beautiful princess I have ever seen,' Eric says, bowing to her in a gentlemanly fashion, making her giggle with glee.

'Hey Tali, wow, you look stunning, wow!'

He stretches out his arms, puts them around me, and gives me a light hug, afraid to mess up my hair, I suppose.

'Thanks, Eric. Coco is beside herself. I think if we don't get started soon, she will burst!' I point to Coco, still jumping up and down in anticipation.

'Well, we're all ready, just waiting for you,' he says and extends his left arm so that I can link my right arm into it.

Slowly, we make our way out of the spare room in the De Lucas' house, now converted into a changing room for the day. We walk through the living area to wait by the large sliding doors that lead to the patio, pool, and garden.

I straighten my dress, made of very light silver satin with silver lace and tiny beads embroidered on the bodice. I had it designed with a gentle sweetheart neckline in the front and back, and cap sleeves that extend from the bodice as a broad band around the middle of my upper arms. A train flows from the softly falling skirt that widens slightly from the bodice as it reaches the floor, just covering my silver sandals.

The doors open, and Eric, in his cream pants and a light shirt, motions to Coco to start walking, and soon after, we follow behind her. We reach the garden area next to the pool, where the guests wait seated at their tables. All the tables are covered in silver tablecloths, the cutlery tied together with cream ribbons. A piece of driftwood, decorated with brightly colored flowers and bits of greenery in between, sits in the center of each table. A huge marquee covers the tables, keeping everyone cool and out of the hot April sun.

Coco bounces off along the grass carpet that runs down between the tables, in a combination of slow motion and trotting, as she throws petals from her basket up into the air and watches as they fall to the ground each time. She delights in the fall of every petal, making the guests laugh and wave at her, admiring her with every step she takes.

Eric and I start walking down the grass carpet as the choir from the orphanage and the church's youth begin to sing, and the guests rise. As we walk, I look around at the people that mean so much to me, who have been my confidants, my shoulders on which to laugh and cry. Cheri and Tian, with Tian Jnr standing between them on a chair, trying to get a better view. Sondra, heavily pregnant with their first child, balances on Neville's arm and Gina and Jurie next to them, smiling widely. As I look to my left, I see June, Suzie, Greg, and Brett together with their partners, and the person who warms my heart most of all is Booker, standing next to his wife, Ruth. He smiles and touches his chest with his right hand, then points to me. I smile at him and nod slightly in recognition and confirmation. I look to my right again, at the table in front of Cheri's. I see Garth and

Merle holding Cole Jnr as he waves at me and blows me kisses. Jackie catches my eye as she looks at Minister Wade standing up front, and she clutches their one-month-old daughter, Natasha. Judith, her eyes focused on Eric, now her fiancé, glances at me quickly, before her attention is drawn back to the man she completely and utterly adores.

Almost at the front, Eric stops, releases my arm, and kisses me lingeringly on the cheek.
'I love you, sis, with all my heart.' Then he turns and gives my arm to the man with whom I am about to spend the rest of my life.
'You take care of her,' he says and smiles as he shakes Josh's hand and goes to take his place next to Judith.
I walk the last few steps with Josh, who cannot take his eyes away from mine.
'You are so beautiful,' he says over and over again, as an almost-invisible tear makes its way down his cheek.
Finally, we are in front of Minister Wade, who has the broadest smile on his face I have ever seen. Josh and I turn to face each other, our hands gripped tightly together. Josh raises my right hand to his lips and ever so softly kisses the engagement ring from Cole, which I am wearing on my right index finger.
'Uh-uh, none of that until I say so!' Minister Wade says aloud, breaking the intimate moment and causing the guests to snicker and us to laugh nervously.

This incredibly handsome man stands before me, immaculately dressed as always, in cream pants and a cream shirt that casually hangs loose, with nothing but love in his eyes. As I stare back, I reminisce about how, from the night at the charity dinner, our friendship grew until he finally mustered the courage at the skydiving teambuilding event to ask me out on our first official date. We went to a theater production of *Annie Get Your Gun*, and after a few more dates, we had our first kiss in the back garden of my house on a warm spring evening. I knew then that I never wanted him to stop kissing me. The first time he told me how much he loved me was as we sat on the beach together, watching a sunset a few weeks later. He told me that, from the day we met, he had felt a tug at his heart and wanted to be at least friends with me. When he proposed at a New Year's Eve party held at his house, in front of all our friends and family, I can't stop staring at this man who is standing in front of me, the man that I completely and utterly love.

As Minister Wade speaks about love, truth, and honesty, I look at Coco as she bounces off to sit on Mr. De Luca's lap, and Mrs. De Luca fusses over her hair and dress. I think back to the day we told them we wanted to adopt Coco, how happy they were, how happy they are with the union of Josh and me. Then I look at my mum. She smiles at me, her eyes filled with love and happiness and tears that bring a lump to my throat. A cheerful giver who has always been my pillar of strength in any situation, I am so blessed to have a mother like her. I once said I only wanted my father's genes, but I was wrong. I need both my father's and my mum's.

A tear rolls down my cheek at the same time as one rolls down my mum's.
How can a mother have so much love to give?
Hers is endless, and her love of God abounds, and she loves me. I smile back at her. She knows how much I love her. She knows that there are not enough words that could explain how much love I have for her, and how we both desperately long for my father to have been here, now, on this blessed day.

Minister Wade brings my attention back to the moment as we begin to say our vows, wholly engrossed in one another, forgetting that there are other people present around us. It is as if we're suspended in an air of togetherness where no one else exists.
'You may kiss the bride,' he announces, and Josh leans forward as I reach for him.
A kiss seals our life together, and for us, this is just the beginning.

I have loved before, and through this love and loss, a few souls have been added to God's kingdom and His service. God has taken me on a journey, and I must ride along with a partner equally passionate about doing good works that please God. Among the people I love and who love me back, I realize that God opens doors. We must walk through them to find the path He wishes for us to take, and in everything, give glory to God.

It is not for us to ask questions but purely to do the Will of God.

<u>***YOUR OPINION***</u>*:*

You've reached the end of this story; I truly hope you enjoyed it and that it touched your heart.

Please be kind and leave your review for the benefit of those who will follow. I will be so appreciative.

https://www.amazon.com/dp/B0073OTPAW

Thank you
God bless you

Aileen Friedman

MORE BOOKS BY THE AUTHOR

Aileen Friedman

When is My Forever
ISBN   978-0-620-55793-1

Second is Best
ISBN   978-0-620-59758-6

The Sparkle in Her Eyes plus Six more Short Stories
ISBN   978-0-620-64434-1

The day God came to earth.
ISBN   978-0-620-68628-0

Radar Love
ISBN   978-1-543-29950-2

Mr. Trolley Adventurer
ISBN   978-1-533-27328-4

Jamie's Discoveries
ISBN   978-1-533-27339-0

The Secret of Grace
ISBN   978-1-719-17242-4